Building
READING
CONFIDENCE
in Adolescents

Building
READING
CONFIDENCE
in Adolescents

*Key Elements That
Enhance Proficiency*

Holly **Johnson**

Lauren **Freedman**

Karen F. **Thomas**

CORWIN PRESS
A SAGE Company
Thousand Oaks, CA 91320

173683698   2-25-08

For information:

Corwin Press
A SAGE Company
2455 Teller Road
Thousand Oaks, California 91320
www.corwinpress.com

SAGE Ltd.
1 Oliver's Yard
55 City Road
London, EC1Y 1SP
United Kingdom

SAGE India Pvt. Ltd.
B 1/I 1 Mohan Cooperative
    Industrial Area
Mathura Road, New Delhi 110 044
India

SAGE Asia-Pacific Pte. Ltd.
33 Pekin Street #02-01
Far East Square
Singapore 048763

Printed in the United States of America

Library of Congress Cataloging-in-Publication Data

Johnson, Holly, 1956-
Building reading confidence in adolescents: key elements that enhance proficiency/Holly Johnson, Lauren Freedman, Karen F. Thomas.
    p. cm.
Includes bibliographical references and index.
ISBN 978-1-4129-5352-8 (cloth)
ISBN 978-1-4129-5353-5 (pbk.)
  1. Reading (Secondary) 2. Teenagers—Books and reading. I. Freedman, Lauren, 1946- II. Thomas, Karen (Karen F.) III. Title.

LB1632.J64 2008
428.4071'2—dc22

2007040311

This book is printed on acid-free paper.

07 08 09 10 11 10 9 8 7 6 5 4 3 2 1

Acquisitions Editor:	Jean Ward
Managing Editor:	Hudson Perigo
Editorial Assistants:	Cassandra Harris, Lesley Blake
Production Editor:	Appingo Publishing Services
Cover Designer:	Rose Storey
Graphic Designer:	Karine Hovsepian

Contents

Acknowledgments

This text could not have been written without the help of those teachers and students in Kentucky, Michigan, and Texas who willingly gave their time to answer our questions. While you anonymously gave of yourselves, through our visits to your classrooms and into your thoughts about reading and self-efficacy, you will remain imprinted on our minds. We can still see you thoughtfully contemplating what validates and violates reading proficiency, and from your careful answers, we now contemplate how to thoughtfully employ your ideas in future classrooms. Thank you is just not enough.

We also wish to acknowledge all of the folks at Corwin who helped us pull this text together. Hudson, Cassandra, and Belinda, we want to thank you for all of your hard work, attention to detail, and quick responses to our queries. This book would not be what it is without you!

About the Authors

Holly Johnson is an associate professor in the Division of Teacher Education at the University of Cincinnati, where she teaches adolescent literacy courses for students interested in becoming middle school teachers. Her research focuses on adolescent literacy and literature and issues of social justice. She taught middle school language arts and social studies in Kentucky and Arizona and was an industrial arts teacher in Botswana, Africa, as a Peace Corps Volunteer.

Lauren Freedman is a professor of literacy studies at Western Michigan University. Her primary areas of expertise include the role of self-efficacy in literacy development, the use of multiple materials within and across the curriculum, inquiry as a framework for instruction and literacy strategy development, and the role of student-led, small group discussion within learning-centered classroom communities.

Karen F. Thomas has been a classroom instructor and administrator in elementary, middle, and high schools for fifteen years, teaching reading and English in urban, public, private, and overseas settings before her current teaching position at the college level. Currently, Thomas is a professor of literacy education at Western Michigan University, where she teaches undergraduate and graduate classes, serves as director of the Dorothy J. McGinnis Reading Center and Clinic, and edits *Reading Horizons*. She also is involved with a number of community initiatives for literacy as part of the Western Michigan University's Clinic Outreach Program as well as coinvestigator for an Early Reading First $3.4 million grant working with Head Start populations.

Introduction

When adolescents walk down school hallways, they display a number of enthusiastic characteristics that may not transfer to the content classroom or to their classroom reading and learning. Boisterous and passionate, many are gregarious, laughing easily at themselves and their friends' antics. Others display their energy through good-natured roughhousing, letting each other know they are part of and accepted as a member of the group. Others walk in pairs, fervently sharing secrets and confidences that only close friendships allow. Still others flash smiles and short waves to one another as they proceed hurriedly toward their next class or extracurricular engagement.

The adolescents with whom we work are in varying stages of the process of becoming active and productive members of our communities and societies, and enthusiasm for life and learning is the foundation of that potential. On the outside, most appear confident, independent, and aware of themselves and the role they play in their clubs, their families, and their friendships. Yet many harbor academic insecurities that are often hidden from their teachers, their peers, and their parents. Afraid to admit their lack of proficiency, they may hide behind the same behaviors we find so engaging in some circumstances. Only through close observation can we begin to see if the secondary students with whom we all work have reading issues that can cause them havoc in their academic lives and anxiety over their future. It is from such close scrutiny that this book was created.

Working with teachers in a Michigan school district to develop inquiry-based instruction using text sets of multiple materials within content classrooms, Lauren observed a variety of student-learning behaviors. Discussing her observations with Robin, the district's language arts/social studies curriculum coordinator, the two focused on several students they had just observed in one of the classrooms. Moving past the realm of cognitive issues that frequently keep teachers in knots in relation to their students' capabilities, Robin and Lauren began to wonder about the more elusive characteristics of learning and teaching that involved student attitude, teacher expectation, and student and classroom material interactions. As they pondered what they had seen, Lauren and Robin focused more and more on the students' responses to the materials accessible to them for the science projects they were creating. Lauren noted that one of the students she observed could not wait to get his hands on the new texts his teacher had brought into the classroom. When given time to browse such materials, he selected several books, went back to his table, opened the first book, went to the table of contents, found a section on whales, turned to those pages, and began to read, jotting down information in his double-entry journal. When asked about his work, he promptly responded that he loved whales and wanted to read everything he could about them. He said that someday he wanted to go whale watching like he had seen on TV.

Another student, however, waited for the teacher to direct her to the books and suggest one. When the student returned to her seat, Lauren noticed that she was not engaged with the book on any level. When asked about her interest and what she was learning, the young girl replied, "Nothing. I hate to read." When pushed by the teacher to just look at the illustrations for ideas that would help her with her project, the adolescent grudgingly complied. Talking with Lauren, the young girl acknowledged that she liked fish and really wanted an aquarium. Once she made this connection, she was more willing to focus on the information available from the captions and the pictures she had in her hands.

Discussing with Robin the discrepancies between these two students' approaches to the activity of the classroom, Lauren noted four recurring elements: *confidence, independence, metacognition,* and *stamina*. The first student seemed to demonstrate confidence, independence, metacognition, and stamina, while the second student seemed to lack them. Lauren then shared her thoughts with Holly and Karen, and together we began to discuss these four elements, noting that while they were not new concepts, they certainly were not addressed often enough in teacher preparation classrooms or in professional development seminars for teachers. Holly suggested that these four concepts seem to be related to self-efficacy, and we began to view them as four concepts necessary to learners' literacy success in academic settings. We further agreed the exploration of students' reading self-efficacy was worthy of pursuing. This text is the result of that pursuit.

■ THE IMPORTANCE OF SELF-EFFICACY IN SECONDARY READING

The connection of self-efficacy to reading has been addressed in terms of competence (M. Smith & Wilhelm, 2004), motivation (Gambrell, 1996), and affect (Frager, 1993; Wang, 2000). Other factors such as self-determination (Angell & Bates, 1996) and confidence (Katims & Harmon, 2000) are also related to the concept of self-efficacy and its connection to literacy. Yet none of these elements completely encompasses the concept of self-efficacy, nor addresses its critical importance to any academic reading event.

Self-efficacy, as described by Bandura (1986), is a person's belief that she or he has the capability to organize and execute the procedures required to control or manage prospective situations. Self-efficacy is not self-concept, however, which Bandura asserted corresponds to a cognitive appraisal that individuals hold about themselves and which crosses dimensions. Often it includes an evaluative statement or judgment of self-worth about the sum total of the individual, not the context-specific behaviors or particular talents the individual possesses. Self-efficacy, however, is limited to a specific context and is an assessment of the competence an individual has to perform a precise task.

Another related concept is confidence, which is an aspect of self-efficacy, but is not a synonym for it. Confidence, like self-concept is not context specific, but rather a general belief about one's capabilities. It is often determined by strength of conviction, which can be either positive or negative, and may not correspond to a precise task. Thus confidence is very much like self-concept, both are general attributes and refer to the whole person, and do not necessarily correspond to a particular task such as reading.

When considering a reading event, self-efficacy corresponds to the reader's belief that he or she can (1) access the appropriate schema; (2) adjust his or her stance toward the text; (3) recognize the purpose for the reading; and then (4) proceed by decoding, comprehending, and using appropriate fix-it strategies necessary to negotiate the text under study. Bandura (1986) further reflected that self-efficacy influences the choices made, the effort initiated, the persistence executed in the face of obstacles, and the affective dimension in reference to the endeavor undertaken. Thus when addressing self-efficacy in relation to reading, what students believe about their capabilities to negotiate a text will effect what choices they make in reference to strategy usage, time spent on the task, effort put into comprehending a text that may be outside their area of comfort or knowledge, and their feelings about what they are reading, or in fact, doing. Self-efficacy encompasses both the cognitive and the affective domains involved in the reading event, and thus should not be overlooked when teaching reading or when asking students to use texts for their learning.

Because many young people approach the task of reading as a difficult or challenging task, educators might well address self-efficacy as explicitly as some of the comprehension strategies they teach their students. The reason for this explicit acknowledgement lies with the reality that "[a] strong sense of efficacy enhances human accomplishment and personal well-being in many ways. People with high assurance in their capabilities approach difficult tasks as challenges to be mastered rather than as threats to be avoided" (Bandura, 1994, p. 71). Reading is a skill that is required of most people regardless of their occupation, and it benefits them in countless ways throughout their days, and their lives. Yet if they fear reading because they lack the assurance that they can process the ink spots on a page (Rosenblatt, 1938, 1998), then they have not been given the most necessary tool to succeed in the world, whether we consider that tool reading or self-efficacy itself.

Bandura (1986) asserted that there are four key processes that help develop self-efficacy; these four elements are (1) mastery experience, (2) vicarious experience, (3) verbal persuasion, and (4) physiological states. Through modeling challenging but accomplishable tasks, verbal encouragement, and strategy instruction, teachers are in the perfect position to increase reading self-efficacy in their students. How they do this is a matter of knowing what types of activities, ways of being, or classroom engagements might best produce results that would motivate young people to persist in reading even as they find the task more challenging than comfortable. We find, however, that self-efficacy itself may be made up of particular elements that would be more concrete and manageable in the classroom environment.

From our readings on self-efficacy, we suggest that four concepts might well be addressed when asking any reader—but especially reluctant or struggling readers—to undertake a reading task. These four elements are a reader's (1) confidence, (2) reading independence, (3) metacognitive awareness, and (4) reading stamina. While at first glance these concepts may seem too abstract to teach, in this text we address how teachers can work with their adolescent students to not only develop the cognitive tasks that content reading demands, but also the affective elements that students bring to that reading.

■ THE PURPOSE OF THE TEXT

Excited by the information we gathered from over 120 teachers and 300 students, we share what we have come to understand about adolescents and reading self-efficacy, especially the concepts of confidence, independence, metacognitive ability, and stamina. Addressing both teacher understandings and student needs, we discuss classroom conditions and practices that can create more proficient readers in Grades 6 to 12.

Knowing how important reading proficiency becomes as students progress in secondary content areas, we explore elements such as the classroom environment, teacher-student interactions, and relationships. We also present particular curricular issues and reading strategies, making a strong case for attending to students' stance or affect in relation to reading. Knowing that the self-efficacy elements we highlight may not be easily taught, we assert that there are, however, particular processes and practices that can create readers who are more proficient, confident, and independent, and aware of their strengths and challenges in connection to the written and visual materials they use in their secondary classrooms.

This text also focuses on the reality that cognition and affect should not be separated from one another, especially in classroom situations. Our research also suggests that the four self-efficacy elements we discuss in this text should not be seen as isolated concepts, but rather part of an ever-increasing spiral that circles back and gathers energy and strength from each of the four elements we discuss. Therefore, readers of the text will find that through building a student's confidence, they are also developing that student's reading independence and stamina as well. And when addressing student stamina, teachers may wish to also utilize processes that will also heighten their students' metacognitive abilities as well. Thus the purpose of this text is to encourage secondary teachers and their students as they work together to produce more proficient readers and ultimately more productive citizens.

THE AUDIENCE FOR THIS TEXT ■

As we worked with secondary teachers from Michigan, Kentucky, and Texas, we continuously thought about how our discoveries would be of interest to other teachers who wondered how to help their own secondary students. Thus this text is written for those teachers. As we continue our research with other teachers and students in different states and different school districts, we find that more of them respond with "aha" moments expressed in such statements as "I knew this was important, but I just sort of forgot as I became more and more immersed in what I was doing" or "How could I not have noticed that feelings students bring to their reading are just as important as their ability to read?" With these reactions in mind, along with the help we received from the teachers and students with whom we worked, this text was brought to fruition to serve as a guide for teachers, teacher educators, and teacher candidates who are interested in developing secondary students' reading self-efficacy through literacy events and engagements in their content areas.

OUTLINE OF THE TEXT ■

In Chapter 1, we present the theory behind our practical ideas about developing reading self-efficacy. Furthermore, we share how our four self-efficacy elements of confidence, independence, metacognitive ability, and stamina connect with the cognitive element of the reading process itself. We define each of the four elements and then share the research that correlates to that element. We also briefly discuss the methods we used in our study of teacher and student ideas about reading self-efficacy.

In Chapter 2, we discuss the concept of confidence. We present teachers' ideas about the processes and practices that they believe will develop more confident readers and then juxtapose these ideas to student responses to our inquiries about confidence. We then provide practical ways in which teachers can encourage the growth of more confident readers.

In Chapter 3, we discuss the concept of independence. Much has been written about creating independent readers, yet we present teachers' and students' ideas of what they believe will make more self-sufficient readers at the secondary level.

Metacognitive ability is the focus of Chapter 4, which we find may be the self-efficacy element most often taught in schools through particular strategies. Metacognition involves self-knowledge, yet often students do not know how to explicitly articulate what they know and how they know it. Such self-knowledge is crucial in becoming more proficient in any activity, yet often we teach the strategies without actually teaching the concept under which the strategies belong. In this chapter, along with specific strategies and attention to classroom environmental factors, we also present ways to help young people become more aware of their reader selves.

Reading stamina is the topic of Chapter 5. Reading stamina is not a concept that is covered much in the literature on reading. For us, reading stamina is more than time on task, it is the ability to persevere in challenging situations. When young adults encounter a text that may be difficult for them, stamina keeps them from closing the book and giving up. From our work with teachers and students, we discovered a number of ways to help secondary readers increase their stamina.

Chapter 6 describes how teachers can create instructional frameworks that utilize an interweaving of the four self-efficacy elements in the pursuit of more proficient readers. We highlight the importance of developing a classroom environment that heightens readers' self-efficacy while also addressing which particular strategies might be used to address confidence and metacognition or independence and stamina. Through a curriculum that uses methods and materials that attend to all four elements in conjunction, teachers provide the opportunity for their secondary students to become the type of readers who are more engaged with classroom activities and more productive as learners.

Throughout the text, we attempt to stay focused on the realities of teachers' lives, the contexts in which they teach, and the types of students with whom they work. Because our work has taken us to a variety of educational settings—from urban centers to rural Texas towns miles from a shopping center or movie theater—this text provides practical solutions to all types of classroom situations. It is our hope that the engagements and suggestions we have presented in this text prove useful to those who work with the delightful adolescents that fill our nation's secondary classrooms.

1

The Four Elements of Reading Self-Efficacy

Many secondary students readily acknowledge that their teachers expect them to read and have tried multiple practices to develop their reading abilities. What causes teachers frustration, however, is why students resist reading and continue to do so despite all the teachers' attempts to build their students' cognitive abilities. Our belief is that we may need to think beyond the cognitive to the more affective domain of reading for content acquisition—to go beyond just the ability to read and to delve more deeply into what readers bring to the reading event or situation in terms of self-efficacy.

In this chapter, we introduce and discuss **C-I-M-S**, a literacy framework based upon the four self-efficacy elements of *c*onfidence, *i*ndependence, *m*etacognition, and *s*tamina and their interrelatedness with the four cueing systems in reading. We developed this framework through our work with middle-grade teachers and students in their classrooms, in professional development meetings, and from extensive readings of research that focused on secondary readers, reading proficiency, and classroom practices and processes that would enhance adolescents' engagement with written texts.

Discussing first the four self-efficacy elements and the literature related to these elements, we share how these elements are connected to the cognitive requirements of the reading process. We discuss how we worked with teachers and students to discover their thinking about practices and processes that can produce confident readers who employ strategies independently as they monitor their reading. We then end with a discussion about categories we created in response to the teacher and student information, which helped us to think about particular aspects of the classroom environment, teacher-student interactions, and curriculum that would benefit secondary readers as they become more proficient readers of the texts they need to read in their content-area classrooms.

■ IDENTIFYING THE SELF-EFFICACY ELEMENTS OF C-I-M-S

Literature on literacy and learning has addressed connections between student learning and confidence, independence, metacognition, and stamina. When we began to explore the idea of reading self-efficacy, we wondered about the structuring of the four self-efficacy elements we observed or did not observe in secondary students: C-I-M-S. From our reading, thinking, and discussing of these elements, we created a framework for studying the impact of C-I-M-S on student literacy development and learning. The significance of facilitating students' development of C-I-M-S is aptly captured in the National Assessment of Educational Progress scores on reading, where students are still not progressing at the rate desired or predicted by those who have created programs to enhance reading skills and strategies.

As we stated in the introduction, self-efficacy is a person's belief that he or she has the capability to do the task set out before him or her (Bandura, 1986). When we first began our study about reading C-I-M-S, we also read about self-efficacy because we thought these four components met the criteria for self-efficacy. Upon reading, we found that Bandura asserted the following conditions create self-efficacy:

- *Mastery experience.* Experiences where one feels in control of the circumstance or feels it can be accomplished successfully.
- *Vicarious experience.* Seeing others similar succeeding at the same experience one is attempting.
- *Verbal persuasion.* Encouragement by others when attempting a particular task.
- *Physiological states.* Positive feelings about the experience or task at hand as well as positive feelings about one's capabilities.

In relation to reading, a person's self-efficacy influences the choice of material the reader selects, the effort the reader puts into the reading task, the ability to persevere in the face of reading challenges, and the way the reader feels about the material he or she is reading and task he or she is to undertake in relation to that reading. Furthermore, self-efficacy conditions what a person believes about his or her ability to comprehend a text, the strategies that person uses when reading, and the purpose for the reading.

Our reading on the four elements only reinforced the concept of our contention of reading self-efficacy, and allowed us to develop definitions for reading confidence, independence, metacognition (or metacognitive ability), and stamina. Those definitions and examples, along with a brief discussion of the literature on those elements, follow.

Confidence

From our readings on confidence, we created the following definition. Confidence is the learner's strength or belief about a capability, in this case the learner's reading ability. Confidence can be measured in terms of success or failure. Two examples are given to show both success and failure:

- If I read about these different weather patterns, I'm pretty sure I'll be able to figure this material out; and
- I'm pretty confident I will fail this class if I don't write a decent paper.

Confidence is not a cognitive skill that can be developed by persistent practice or direct instruction. Rather it is an affective element that influences students' cognitive abilities and academic performances. Georgiou (1999) suggested that while many students are capable of high academic performances, for many, their feelings about themselves may get in the way of their learning. Tavani and Losh (2003) contended that a student has intellectual self-confidence and social self-confidence and that both have strong relationships to literacy development.

Frank Pajares (2004) asserted, "Self-efficacy beliefs...influence the *choices* people make and the courses of actions they pursue. Individuals tend to select tasks and activities in which they feel competent and confident and avoid those in which they do not" (p. 2). Thus struggling readers who lack the assurance that engaging in a text will lead to comprehension and feel confident that reading will *not* be beneficial to them continue to have decreasing self-worth because literacy is so important in our society (McCray, 2001).

Independence

Independence is the ability to pursue an endeavor without the help of another. Our definition is the following: Independence is the ability to apply a specific literacy strategy after determining the literacy demands without the aid of another. For example,

- this is a great book on weather, but I need to look up what it has on tornadoes in the index.

Literacy educators strive to bring about independence in their students. Historically, our society values independence as an attribute and values the rights that frequently accompany the concept: freedom, choice, and opportunity. Building from the foundation of freedom, choice, and opportunity, which would be considered aspects of independent readers, literacy proponents also address motivation (Gambrell, 1996; Tovani & Losh, 2003) and fluency (Worthy & Broaddus, 2002). Independence, however, is often procured by first scaffolding students as they learn to negotiate more difficult texts, writing genres, or different text structures and formats. Through methods and models that gradually release responsibility (Pearson & Gallagher, 1983) to students, teachers facilitate the move to independent literacy usage and production. What it means to be independent might best be thought of as a developmental process more than an a priori state.

Metacognition

The third self-efficacy element in the C-I-M-S model, metacognition, is defined by Harris and Hodges (1995) as the "awareness and knowledge of one's mental processes such that one can monitor, regulate, and direct [one] to a desired end; self-mediation" (p. 153). For ease, we created the following: Metacognition is the learner's awareness of what he or she knows and what he or she does not know including what is needed to find out the unknown. For example,

- This pie chart on weather will allow me to learn what I need to know, but I need to first learn how to read a pie chart.

Metacognitive awareness is crucial in monitoring personal reading, viewing, and writing strategies as well as the processes used when producing texts. Metacognition allows a reader or writer to know that text should make sense and that when it does not, he or she needs to make choices and act upon those choices. In this way, metacognition constitutes knowledge of the self, the kinds of literacy tasks we engage in, and strategies we use while engaged in tasks (Baker & Brown, 1984; Garner, 1994).

Metacognitive knowledge, as it relates to reading, has been organized into three subcategories: procedural, conditional, and declarative knowledge (Billingsley & Wildman, 1990; Jacobs & Paris, 1987; Paris, Lipson, & Wixon, 1983). Procedural knowledge is an awareness of process necessary to complete a strategy or task. This involves a student knowing *how* to use context, *how* to discern main ideas from details, or *how* to sequence events for chronology. Students have procedural knowledge if they know about specific strategies, can select the appropriate one, and know how to employ it. Conditional knowledge involves readers knowing *"why* strategies are effective, *when* they should be applied and *when* they are appropriate"* (Jacobs & Paris, 1987). Declarative knowledge involves the three aspects of metacognitive knowledge from Flavell's (1979) work: task, strategy, and person. This knowledge focuses on readers' beliefs and on what they know about the characteristics of the text, the reading task, themselves as learners, and possible strategies that can be employed.

Stamina

For stamina, we explored dictionary definitions as well as synonyms that teachers would consider in relation to literacy. Our definition evolved into the following: Stamina is the learner's perseverance and pacing of him- or herself when a task may become difficult or last longer than expected. For example,

- I will check out the hurricane information across these texts to make sure that what I have is complete and accurate even though it may take longer than I wanted.

There is little in the literature addressing stamina. There are, however, related studies addressing the *concept* of stamina through the efficacy elements that impact and result in stamina in the literacy process. Engagement is one such element and Au (1997) indicated that ownership and self-confidence result in engagement and engagement results in increased stamina. Berliner and Biddle (1995) and Tobin (1984) asserted that learners engaged in literacy tasks based on the concept of on-task behavior, which is one aspect of stamina.

We find stamina an important self-efficacy issue in literacy learning, especially when we see numbers of learners not being able to complete extended literacy tasks. Students frequently "fall apart" when state testing or other lengthy assessments are assigned. Many students are capable of success in some literacy demands but have never been given the opportunities to engage for sustained periods in tasks calling for engaged behavior such as reading longer texts or writing over an extended period. Noting that stamina is often considered only as an aspect of time-on-task, we suggest that stamina also consists of perseverance and the ability to stick with a task when the learner feels there is difficulty involved.

Ultimately, literacy self-efficacy results from the combination of confidence, independence, metacognitive awareness, and stamina. Determining that literacy self-efficacy is the interrelatedness of these four elements over others, such as intention or motivation, we noted that motivation and intention drive behaviors already affected by confidence, independence, metacognition, and stamina, which lead to differing proficiencies in literacy learning, consumption, and production. We also explored the concepts of interest and desire, but also felt that these characteristics that the learner brings to a literacy event are conditioned by the four efficacy elements we identified.

From our readings and discussions, we realized that instructional processes, practices, and learning conditions impact directly on these efficacy elements. Self-efficacy encompasses both cognitive and affective domains involved in a literacy event and, thus, teachers should not overlook it when teaching or asking students to use, consume, or create texts for their learning.

SELF-EFFICACY AND THE CUEING SYSTEMS ■

We also recognized that the four self-efficacy elements of C-I-M-S build on one another and are interconnected with the four cueing systems of literacy. In Figure 1.1, we present our model showing how the self-efficacy elements of C-I-M-S are interrelated to the four cueing systems: (1) graphophonic (sound-word relationship), (2) syntactic (sentence order or grammar), (3) semantic (words and their combinations creating meaning), and (4) pragmatic (purpose or function of the literacy event).

As Figure 1.1 illustrates, the inner circle produced by the cueing systems and the outer circle containing the self-efficacy elements are joined by a perforated line. This suggests that what students bring to the cognitive event of the literacy process can influence the process itself. For instance, if a reader is not confident in her ability to decode the text (using the graphophonic cueing system), then she may resist reading altogether, thus limiting her access to the content available to her. Other examples might be when a writer lacks the metacognitive awareness of writing for a purpose, or that writers create ideal audiences for themselves when writing. Without such awareness, the pragmatic cueing system may not be engaged. In another example, students who are just learning English as an additional language may feel they cannot independently author a text, whether through a reading transaction (Rosenblatt, 1938) or writing engagement. Their syntactic proficiency may keep them from attempting to write or read the texts required. Thus they may feel they cannot complete a task when asked to do so. Additionally, students who do not have the stamina to remain engaged in a literacy task may miss the meaning they could make from a text.

Figure 1.1
The Four Efficacy Elements and the Four Cueing Systems

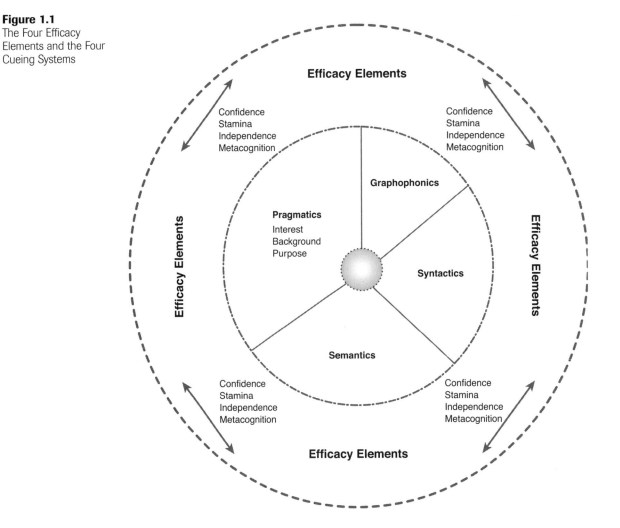

Through our dialogues and study of C-I-M-S, we have come to recognize that they are foundational to successful utilization of the cueing systems. And while our examples show each of the efficacy elements in relation to only one of the cueing systems, we suggest that we have also come to realize that when teachers invite learners to engage in a literacy event (reading, writing, speaking/listening, and thinking), they must also consider students' self-efficacy or C-I-M-S strength. Furthermore, we need to support development of this strength to access the graphophonology, syntax, semantics, and pragmatics of an event. Kucer (2005) suggested that there are four dimensions of a literacy event: (1) cognitive, (2) linguistic, (3) sociocultural, and (4) developmental. Our model connecting C-I-M-S to the cueing systems proposes that C-I-M-S is based on literacy being socially constructed and mediated by teacher, learner, text, and task (Dewey, 1918;

Piaget, 1973; Vygotsky, 1978). Literacy events are also developmental, and "each act of literacy reflects those aspects of literacy that the individual does and does not control in any given context" (Kucer, 2005, p. 6). The understanding of the literacy self-efficacy that each learner brings to a literacy event and making such knowledge explicit creates the possibility for fulfilling all the dimensions of language that Kucer highlighted: graphemic, graphophonemic, orthographic, morphemic, syntactic, semantic, text structure, genre, text type, and pragmatic.

LEARNING FROM TEACHERS AND STUDENTS ■

After we reviewed over seventy research reports and journal articles to develop our definitions (as previously reported), we wanted to know what teachers and students had to say about each of the four efficacy elements. Baumann and Duffy-Hester (2002) suggested, "Methodology for teacher researchers involves their beliefs about the world of teaching, learning, children, and classroom life. Methods, *in contrast*, are the procedures and tools a researcher employs in an inquiry" (p. 2). We want to report both our methodology and our methods so that others could also conduct this research with those in their schools or districts since the particular answers for their students and teachers may differ from what we have found in our study with teachers in Michigan, Texas, and Kentucky.

This project revolved around our belief that C-I-M-S is a viable model for successful, effective readers. We were convinced from our own teaching of middle school students as well as our thinking and discussions with each other that teachers can make a difference in the reading lives of their students. Our reading of the literature also solidified our thinking, but once we had explored the literature on confidence, independence, metacognition, and stamina, we wondered what teachers thought about the idea of self-efficacy in connection to literacy learning. Since we lived in different areas of the country as well as worked with teachers in other parts of the state and country, we decided to get a wide sample of teacher and student thought. We asked 107 teachers and 330 students the following three questions about each one of the C-I-M-S elements:

- What does it mean to have [C-I-M-S] in connection to literacy?
- What practices or conditions validate the development of [C-I-M-S] in relation to literacy?
- What practices or conditions violate the development of [C-I-M-S] in relation to literacy?

A fourth question we asked students on each of the questionnaires was whether or not they had confidence, independence, metacognitive ability, or stamina, and why or why not.

In addition to these questionnaires, we observed many of these same teachers in their classrooms, interviewed some of them about the idea of reading self-efficacy, and then reviewed the questionnaires' ratings of confidence, independence, metacognition, and stamina. Because we divided the efficacy elements into four separate questionnaires for each teacher, we ended up with 428 questionnaires (107 on each component) to review. The student data was more difficult to tally because while 330 of them did answer the questionnaires on confidence, the numbers decreased for each of the other questionnaires because of student absence or disinterest. We still ended up with over 270 students answering each of the questionnaires and had over 1,100 questionnaires to examine.

Starting with the teacher questionnaires, we found that there were particular practices that teachers universally felt validated and enhanced secondary readers' self-efficacy while other practices universally disrupted or violated C-I-M-S. As we read through the data, we began to place related concepts and practices together, discussing our ideas as we continued to read. We began separating the ideas into specific categories and eventually developed five large categories: (1) Classroom Environment, (2) Teaching/Learning Dialectic, (3) Curricular Planning, (4) Affective Issues, and (5) Specific Strategies. We placed particular practices within each of the categories according to what the teachers wrote; the description of these categories include the following:

- *Environment:* the physical environment as well as social environment of the classroom space;
- *Teaching/Learning Dialectic:* the ongoing, daily practices that occur between teacher and student as well as student and student;
- *Curricular Planning:* the overall way in which teachers plan to accomplish the learning within the classroom;
- *Affective Issues:* the feelings that accompany the interactions within the classroom between participants; and
- *Specific Strategies:* literacy strategies that teachers listed, such as paired reading, think-alouds, or literature circles (Short, Harste, & Burke, 1996).

We developed these five overall categories because the information the teachers and students shared on the questionnaires were similar enough to fit within those categories. Thus, in Chapters 2–5 where we share the specific information on confidence, independence, metacognition, or stamina, we discuss the particular practices, conditions, strategies, or processes that validated or violated the development of C-I-M-S. Here, however, we present the overall findings from across all the data we collected.

■ VALIDATING AND VIOLATING C-I-M-S

Within each of the five categories we constructed, we had several practices or concepts. By understanding what the teachers and students reported, we have more to consider and to construct in terms of classroom practices and conditions that produce students' literacy self-efficacy.

Validation of Readers' C-I-M-S

Upon analysis of the questionnaires, interviews, and field notes, we found that each of the five categories produced environmental, cognitive, or affective conditions and practices that would validate students' confidence, independence, metacognition, and stamina in relation to literacy learning, consumption, and production. While each of the C-I-M-S elements has particular practices and strategies that will develop or enhance it (discussed in Chapters 2–5) we propose that the four cannot be taught in isolation from either the cognitive aspects of learning or independently of each other. (We further discuss this interconnection in Chapter 6.) Thus we discuss them by means of the five categories we created when we analyzed the data but recognize that the categories often overlap and that the elements may be mentioned in relationship to each other throughout the following discussion. And while we do not have the space to discuss all of the ideas that we list in Chapters 2–5, we do attempt to create a unified picture of what the data and our analysis suggest about increasing students' self-efficacy.

Environmental Elements

We created this category based on the data from the teachers and students that included all elements within each of the other categories combined with language they used such as "relaxed" or "they feel comfortable in the classroom." Our observations of secondary classrooms supported this category since our notes entailed how the physical classroom appeared and how students and teachers interacted with each other. Language such as "comfortable," "responsive," "democratic," and "collaborative" was used to describe the feelings and the processes of the classroom. "Transformative" was one of the words we used because the type of learning that teachers and students suggested would validate students' C-I-M-S would transform students' feelings about themselves and their literacy practices.

Teachers and students felt that if schools could create practices and conditions that allowed students' literacy self-efficacy to flourish, they needed classrooms where students felt they were accepted, their voices were heard, and their input was valuable and acted upon. Furthermore, the literacy processes would have to be authentic, and the literacy processes the students performed in the classroom could be utilized outside of it. Thus, the environment would be authentic. Teachers and students also felt that learning and reading would need to be scaffolded to encourage students' C-I-M-S, and that teaching would be incremental and built upon student interest and prior knowledge. In essence, learning would be more fluid, more organized, and more developmental. Students would feel being in the classroom was easy and that learning was fun but challenging.

Returning to the literature on self-efficacy, we propose that since confidence resides in the affective domain, but influences cognitive development connected with metacognition and independence, teachers need to consider the social cues and environmental situations. Particular environmental behaviors and curricular designs can increase student confidence (Sanacore, 2000; Swafford & Bryan, 2000; Williams, 2001). Workshop environments, affective and cognitive interactions between students and teachers, and practices such as retrospective miscue analysis (Goodman, 1996) develop students' cognitive understanding (metacognitive skills) about their learning processes, which further increases their confidence and their feelings of independence. Once students understand how learning occurs *for them*, which is a metacognitive ability, their confidence gives rise to increased stamina. As Goodman asserted, "Readers' beliefs about themselves as readers often influence their literacy development" (p. 600).

Environmental conditions set the stage for students' beliefs about themselves and their learning. Creating classrooms and learning conditions to foster students' confidence is in the teacher's control.

Teaching/Learning Dialectic

What occurs among the members of a learning environment also plays a role in the development of students' literacy self-efficacy. Practices such as scaffolding learning, connecting to prior knowledge, and making learning more explicit were all aspects of the teaching and learning dialectic that the teachers and students felt were important. Additional practices included creating lessons that allowed for teacher modeling as well as time for students to complete assignments in the classroom where the teacher was there as a support. The teachers also recognized that strategies needed to be integrated into the learning, and not necessarily taught in isolation where students could not transfer the skill or take ownership of the learning in connection to their own work.

Teachers who utilize the gradual release of responsibility (GRR) model of teaching and learning (Pearson & Gallagher, 1983) find that students gain independence through a dialectic that also lets the students be the teachers when they are ready to accept the responsibility for their learning and have the cognitive abilities that will produce the expected results. Activities that have students working with younger children, that create situations where students are able to repeat or redo work, ask for students' input on rubric creation, and include use of their examples for the edification of others are all aspects of teaching and learning that the teachers mentioned in this study. They also saw the need to make the learning process and the "due dates" of longer projects more explicit with their students. Inviting their students into the learning process was the necessary component for teaching. It also encourages more independent learners.

Recognizing that independence is a goal teachers pursue in their literacy teaching, Sanacore (1999) suggested, "Students need opportunities to gain a sense of self-determination" (p. 38). Self-determination can be developed through practices such as silent sustained reading (SSR) with books of interest to the reader, choice in reading materials, and response engagements where the reader selects what to ponder. Students also achieve independence when they are given responsibilities they are able to accomplish (Pearson & Gallagher, 1983; Smith & Johnson, 1993). Thus, classroom organization that provides for student responsibility is also a vital element leading toward learning self-efficacy.

Curricular Decisions

The types of activities, units, and curricular design teachers plan are fundamentally connected to students' learning. In relation to literacy and self-efficacy, the teachers suggested that choice, time for students to learn and think, and ability to work with students to plan units and activities were all key elements in producing literacy self-efficacy. Students supported these ideas, with a special emphasis on choice. The use of multiple materials on all reading levels along with SSR and writing in all content areas were also seen as positive ways to allow students to gain proficiency in literacy learning.

These teachers also believed they needed to plan for teaching the process of discussion along with the time it takes for students to reflect upon their learning either orally or silently and to allow their students to redo tests or other assignments. All of which meant planning their units in more student-friendly or learning-centered ways. The use of an inquiry curriculum, which allows for student choice and student interest (Freedman & Johnson, 2004) was also mentioned in the data. Additionally, teachers also noted the use of technology and units planned to allow for student scaffolding along with connecting the aesthetic aspect of reading to the efferent task often forefronted in content classrooms.

Affective Issues

The affective issues that validate students' self-efficacy are as important as the cognitive and environmental concerns to the teacher participants. One of the most powerful messages we heard addressed the need to listen to students and get to know them as people. Valuing students and their work, while also encouraging them as they learned was another aspect of the affective domain the teachers mentioned. Making sure students could increase their stamina for learning and particular tasks by allowing them breaks and perhaps making sure they had enough nutrition were also mentioned by the teachers along with recognizing that all students can and do learn, and they do so in multiple ways. Other issues had to do with student interactions such as creating ways for students to care about one another and one another's work. Seeing their students as human beings who were apprentices in the learning environment was how we came to understand what these teachers thought would be the best way to help facilitate their students' self-efficacy. Literacy self-efficacy is ultimately about growing toward proficiency within an environment that will allow for self-determination, choice, freedom, and opportunity while also providing a zone of safety (Lipka & McCarthy, 1994) facilitated by caring others.

Strategies

As we read through the data, we noted that particular strategies were listed as beneficial for creating self-efficacy in adolescent literacy learners. The teachers mentioned the use of all of the language arts or communication skills to produce confident and independent literacy learners who could utilize their metacognitive skills over a sustained period or a challenging task. SSR, sustained silent writing, and think-alouds were three strategies that teachers might best plan for and model in their classrooms. Block and Israel (2004) and Oster (2001) suggested that one of the best practices of teacher modeling is the think-aloud, which shows students what proficient literacy learners, consumers, and producers do during literacy events. The C3B4 Me strategy, which asks students to see three others in the classroom community before questioning the teacher, allows students to see each other as having literacy abilities that are beneficial to others. Using quick writes and outlining along with teaching the reading process also builds students' literacy proficiency. Using literature circles

(Short, Harste, & Burke, 1996) and teaching students the difference between debate and discussion also enhance students' confidence and thinking abilities. In essence, these teachers believed that the use of strategies that utilized students' thinking, reading, writing, visualizing, and speaking skills would create self-efficacy in their students.

Upon review of the data, we came to realize that students' literacy self-efficacy develops when teachers engage in practices that build and reinforce in their students (1) a confidence in their capabilities as learners, (2) an independence to pursue learning engagements and strategies, (3) metacognitive ability that helps them recognize their strengths and needs when they proceed through learning tasks, and (4) stamina through a willingness to tackle difficult aspects of a task and pursue it to completion. Students often agreed with the teachers about the conditions, practices, and strategies to use in the classroom and added many of their own ideas. A repertoire of strategies allows literacy self-efficacy development to occur among a variety of learners and learning styles.

Violation of Readers' C-I-M-S

While we wish to remain focused on the practices and processes that validate or encourage the development of students' literacy processes, there were practices and conditions the teachers and students reported that violated students' C-I-M-S. Classroom conditions that were stressful or disruptive violated the development of student literacy processes. Affective elements such as "them and me" dialectic rather than a "we" construct also impinged upon students' C-I-M-S growth.

Further violations of self-efficacy included instances when teachers engaged in practices that created in their students a sense of inability (lack of confidence) that impeded their willingness to engage with classroom content or activity without explicit guidance (lack of independence). Several teachers noted that they often assumed a prior knowledge their students did not have. Other violations they felt disrupted their students' metcognitive ability or strategy use was when they placed too much emphasis on "correctness" and doing everything "the teacher's way." The teachers often felt they did not have the time to allow for student input into assignments or the allowance of learning that may include mistakes such as overgeneralizations or misinterpretation that could readily be addressed with further instruction.

Another practice that the teachers reported was when they did not think through a process they were asking their students to perform or did not assess student strengths or needs before assigning a literacy event such as reading a textbook that may be too difficult or asking their students to write essays on topics that students did not find of interest. The teachers believed that they decreased student stamina when their students saw classroom requirements as too much of a challenge, which created stumbling blocks instead of opportunities to explore and experiment. This connected to the strategies that they felt might limit students' literacy growth.

Strategies that violated students' C-I-M-S included round-robin reading and too much SSR of texts that did not hold the students' interest. Limiting students' engagement with one another in strategies such as paired reading or discussion of their written work also blocked their literacy growth. Too little group work where students could learn from one another was also listed as a practice that violated C-I-M-S. Thus, the lack of literature circles in any of the content areas was seen as violating student confidence, independence, metacognition, and stamina development.

Ultimately, we interpreted comments about practices and conditions that violated C-I-M-S growth as connected to two classroom concerns: (1) the lack of awareness as to the importance of the affective domain when learning, and (2) the lack of time to actually address both the affective and cognitive elements of learning. We see these as two related concerns that are tied to the pressure teachers feel to cover the material they are expected to teach and interwoven with their fears about state testing. The teachers interviewed reported their concern about not addressing student needs, and they understood that schools may be doing more damage than good when it came to "lifelong learning." They did not know how to alleviate their own and the public's emphasis on testing and what that means to them and to their work as teachers, to their schools and communities, and to their state and nation as a whole. As Block (2004) suggested, while we may know more about literacy instruction than at any other time, many classroom teachers still fail to engage students effectively in literacy events.

CONCLUDING COMMENTS ■

Through modeling, challenging but accomplishable tasks, verbal encouragement, and strategy instruction, teachers are in the perfect position to increase students' literacy self-efficacy. When we discussed the four key elements of confidence, independence, metacognition, and stamina that Lauren Freedman first noted in her conversation with Robin, the Language Arts/Literacy Coordinator of a Michigan school district, we could see how they could easily be captured under the umbrella of self-efficacy. As Bandura's (1986) four elements suggested, all students, but especially those who struggle with content area materials in their secondary classrooms, need the practice, teacher modeling, teacher encouragement, and an affective state that will allow their literacy self-efficacy to develop. Along with such development, their cognitive abilities will also increase.

What we have presented in our C-I-M-S model is what we have learned from teachers and their students, and is based on what effective literacy users, consumers, and producers need to be effective and proficient in relation to the literacy tasks they are expected to perform at the secondary level. Ultimately, literacy learning that accommodates students' C-I-M-S allows them to learn efficiently and "effortlessly" (Smith, 1997) about the content in a text and about themselves as users, consumers, and producers of literacy rather than wrestle with self-doubt, self-deprecation, and fear of failure.

2

A Closer Look at Confidence and Reading

Teachers recognize confidence or the lack of it in students by the way they walk through the halls and sit in classrooms. There is something about the way they hold themselves, attempt the tasks set before them, and interact with others in their environment. It is more than self-awareness regarding knowledge or expertise in a particular area, the ability to perform a specific skill, or the way to act in certain social situations. Confidence is much more about attitude and self-knowing than about specific ability or capability. In a school setting, it includes a student's realistic awareness that personal effort or lack of it can produce a result.

Confidence

Confidence is a learner's strength of belief about a capability—in this example, the learner's reading ability. Confidence can be measured in terms of understanding what will insure success or failure.

Examples

1. If I read about these different weather patterns, I'm pretty sure I'll be able to figure out this material.

2. I'm sure I will fail the test if I don't understand the information in this chapter.

Students with confidence are not always those who blurt out the answers right away or take over small group discussions, but they are the ones who attempt to bring their knowledge of themselves and their abilities into the classroom. Development of students' confidence in their approach to reading often has to do with how students, teachers, and the environment interact to bring about a self-knowing that is characterized by students feeling comfortable about who they are and what they might be able to do if given a chance, a choice, and a bit of support along the way.

■ WHAT TEACHERS HAVE TO SAY ABOUT CONFIDENCE AND READING

As previewed in the first chapter, the four identified components of student self-efficacy are confidence, independence, metacognition, and stamina. To examine ways to develop these traits in students, this and future chapters begin with a look at what teachers and students themselves say about how they believe students can grow in this important aspect. Informed by their perspectives, drawn from a sample of one hundred teachers and three hundred students, the chapter then discusses additional research-based strategies that give promise of strengthening the particular aspect of reading self-efficacy under examination. Ways in which over one hundred teachers feel confidence can be developed in middle and secondary school readers appear in Figure 2.1, sorted into the five teaching domains identified in Chapter 1, within which teachers can find ways to help students develop self efficacy in reading. These again are (1) environment, (2) teaching and learning, (3) curriculum planning, (4) affective interactions, and (5) specific strategies. In the case of confidence development, teachers identified aspects of teaching and learning that addressed all five of these areas.

Teaching and Learning

Teaching and learning relationships that help develop reader confidence include a number of teaching strategies that the teacher can implement into any classroom. As the chart in Figure 2.1 shows, there are a number of different everyday teaching strategies teachers can either include in their planning or use spontaneously to help build their students' reading confidence. Two elements teachers find beneficial are having students discuss the assigned readings and having students present products based on their readings.

Furthermore, teachers recognize the importance of discussing the reading that they are requiring in their content classrooms, even though it is sometimes difficult to find the time for this. Even informal conversations that take little time each day can help students build their confidence in their reading abilities for two reasons. The first is that they feel the teacher values their ideas and opinions about the reading, and the second is that, through discussion, students find out whether they understood the readings. When they find that they have understood a piece of difficult text, it increases their confidence. By working with others through dialogue, those who did not understand the reading are not as embarrassed by their lack of understanding, and they have the opportunity to hear how their peers may compare the information to something familiar to them or to hear how others summarize the information, which can help build their knowledge of the content under study.

Environment	Teaching/ Learning	Curricular Decisions	Affective Decisions	Strategies
Supportive Responsive	Discussion of prior knowledge (5)	Choice (15)	No put down policy (4)	Peer tutoring (2)
	Repetition	Book talks (4)	Value all student input (6)	Retelling (24)
	Building connections to students' lives	Scaffolding (4)	Positive comments/ facial expressions (29)	Rehearsed oral
	Present/publish finished products (9)	Open book assessments (2)	Praise student work and effort (7)	Reading (no round robin reading) (22)
	Students reading aloud to younger learners (2)	Redo work or retake assessments (4)	Get to know each student (12)	Literature circles (31)
	Focus on strengths to address needs (6)	Opportunities to take risks (6)	Facilitate students' caring for each other (5)	Say something (4)
	Reading something at independent level (6)	Time for practice (3)	Call on students who have the information (4)	Sharing prior knowledge (2)
	Use of student examples (6)	Opportunities for differing interpretations (4)		Written conversation (20)
	Learners write and tell stories about themselves (4)	Acknowledge teacher mistakes (2)		Previewing (3)
	Sharing and valuing opinions (33)	Model learning as well as knowing (8)		Predicting (3)
	Asking lots of questions (9)	Use of multiple materials (26)		Skimming and Scanning (2)
				Choral reading
				Sharing opinions (2)
				Word wall (22)

Figure 2.1 Confidence: Pedagogical Factors Reported by Teachers (N = 107)

A second teaching and learning element that produces reading confidence is the sharing of finished products that result from the reading teachers require in their classrooms. When teachers ask the students to produce something from their reading, they are asking students to apply their understanding, thereby extending and demonstrating comprehension of the material that has been read. There are three common types of reading comprehension:

- *Literal comprehension:* students state what is written in the texts.
- *Interpretive comprehension:* students may need to infer what the text is suggesting.
- *Applied comprehension:* students use the information in the text.

By asking students to apply the knowledge they garnered from the reading, teachers find that students will increase their reading confidence, since this application means that the students really understood what they read, and that they will often build a deeper understanding.

Curriculum Planning for Enhancing Reading Confidence

When teachers think about curricular planning that enhances reading confidence one of the most important ideas to emerge is that of giving students a choice of reading materials. Choice allows students control over their learning, which can increase their confidence. Connected to choice is the use of multiple materials to cover a content topic. When using multiple materials, teachers allow students to explore particular subtopics, and a variety of opinions, and to read at varying reading levels. Even the most proficient reader may derive benefit from a practice or warm up to reading more difficult or complex texts by first reading at a lower reading level. Together, choice and multiple materials create opportunities for all students to become engaged in classroom reading.

Affective Interactions and Confidence

Examining the affective elements teachers suggest in relation to classroom interactions, the two they list most frequently for creating confidence are (1) teachers knowing their students and (2) teachers providing their students with positive feedback. By learning about their students and what their students' individual reading interests or challenges are, teachers create more positive interactions. These interactions have the potential for increasing student confidence because teachers can use this knowledge to support and respond to their students on a one-to-one basis. Added to this knowledge is the ability to see how the students grow and develop as learners and readers, and to encourage that growth through positive feedback.

Strategies for Building Readers' Confidence

Teachers consider oral reading strongly productive of reading confidence. Many students have difficulty with reading aloud because their confidence has been wounded through these types of experiences, which is detrimental to their growth as readers. Strategies reported in literacy research that incorporate oral reading include literature circles, retellings, and rehearsed oral readings. Literature circles—small groups meeting together to discuss their readings in free-flowing conversations—allow students to more fully form their thoughts and insights (Short, Harste, & Burke, 1996) and build students' confidence because they come to recognize that they understand the reading and feel encouraged when they share their meaning making with others in a "zone of safety" (Lipka & McCarty, 1994). Rehearsed oral readings, whereby students have opportunity to practice and peer coach the reading of a text and then read it aloud with others, accomplish a similar sense of security because students have the opportunity to practice their oral reading skills and to address any pronunciation issues involved in that reading.

■ WHAT STUDENTS HAVE TO SAY ABOUT CONFIDENCE AND READING

In exploring what students believe would enhance their reading confidence, and using the same four categories, students identify ways they believe teachers could help them with their reading proficiency and confidence, as seen in Figure 2.3.

Teaching and Learning

Students are still building their background knowledge for most of the content they are learning. Part of their knowledge base involves vocabulary, and this aspect of reading is the most frequently mentioned by students as a means to acquire reading confidence. The second place where students feel they need the most help is in reading aloud. As we previously mentioned, reading confidence is closely related to oral reading, perhaps because this is where students developed early proficiency or lack thereof. Thus teachers need to address the vocabulary encountered in content reading in ways that will facilitate their students' pronunciation and also deep knowledge of the language their students find in the materials used in the classroom.

Curriculum Planning for Enhancing Reading Confidence

Students feel that reading aloud in small groups improves their reading ability and builds their confidence. When planning for student learning that will increase reading confidence, teachers might begin to think about the use of content area literature circles (Johnson & Freedman, 2005). Content area literature circles are small group discussions that focus on expository texts and content acquisition while also allowing students to discuss the content in a variety of ways that will facilitate individual learning styles. All of the major questions (as seen in Figure 2.2) that students discuss when involved in content area literature circles have importance for their growth as thoughtful readers and consumers of content.

Figure 2.2 Six Questions for Facilitating Content Learning (Johnson & Freedman, 2005)

Content area literature circles are small groups of students who discuss the informational texts used in their content classrooms. Students can be asked the same question, or the teacher may ask different groups to address different questions to facilitate all types of learning when the small groups report to the whole class. The six major questions are the following:

1. What did you learn from this reading? (This is for summarizing skills.)
2. What significant language or vocabulary did you encounter in this reading? (This question addresses vocabulary and concepts in the reading.)
3. What perspective(s) were highlighted in this reading? Which perspective(s) are missing? (These questions ask students to think critically about point of view.)
4. What questions do you now have in connection to this reading? (This question asks students to question pose from the reading and not simply ask questions that can be answered in the text.)
5. What do you think are the most important points of the reading? (This question asks students to think about the key points of the passage.)
6. What problems may result from the information you have encountered in this reading? (This asks students to problem pose in terms of the content itself or to address how the text is written that is not conducive to their understanding.)

A second factor that students identified as a way to increase their reading confidence is having more class time to read. As we know, students read at a variety of levels. They also read at different paces, and this is often difficult to facilitate in content classrooms. Yet teachers also know that many students do not read the materials assigned or read outside of class. Thus teachers find themselves teaching lessons around assigned texts that many students have not read. This reading and teaching behavior is detrimental to students' reading confidence as well as teaching-time utilization.

By planning times for students to just read the content materials, teachers will enhance reading confidence, perhaps even their students' reading fluency, since reading fluency can be developed through reading practice.

Affective Interactions and Confidence

Motivation and encouragement are two elements students believe would make them more confident readers. Because teachers are the most important classroom element, their support and encouragement of students is crucial. Of course, teacher encouragement needs to be authentic. Thus even the way teachers go about complimenting students and giving them feedback becomes another aspect of teaching and the classroom environment that needs to be considered.

Motivation might best be achieved through teacher passion and interest rather than rote external rewards such as candy or small material gifts. There are times, however, when such small gifts may work effectively, but we would suggest they be used sporadically. Encouragement through curricular designs such as inquiry or thematic units that allow and trust students to become responsible for their own learning also boosts confidence. Learning through inquiry or thematic units needs to be scaffolded by the teacher, though, to ensure successful process and content learning so that students gradually become responsible for their own learning and discoveries and not lost on their own in the process.

Figure 2.3
Confidence—
Pedagogical Factors
Reported by Students

Environment	Teaching/ Learning	Curricular Decisions	Affective Decisions	Strategies
	Help students read difficult books/ vocabulary (61)	Reading aloud in a safe atmosphere (home/ small groups, with teacher) (28)	Motivate by praise/ encouragement (39)	Book clubs (4)
	Find right book for each student (11)		Recognize that not all students read on same level	Paired reading (5)
	Goal setting/ purpose (2)	Choice in reading (17)	Don't get angry when we don't know (2)	Sustained silent reading (8)
	Discuss the reading (9)	Limit homework		Choral reading (8)
	Teacher reads aloud (11)	Using interesting/ exciting/ age-related books (12)	Make sure we can read	Using tapes
Collaborative	Read-aloud (practice first) (43)	Book variety (14)	Believe in us (4)	Context clues
Comfortable	Use books on students' instructional level (challenge a little) (24)	Accelerated reading	Rewards (candy) (6)	Rereading
Democratic	Explain import/fun of reading (5)	Make reading more fun (9)	Be there for us (2)	Leveled books (2)
Engaged	Let students use strategies	Time to read at school (45)	Care about us	Interest inventory (2)
	Reading tutors/afterschool tutorials (20)	Teach strategies for understanding (12)	Quiet during reading	"What if . . ."
	Read more each day (3)	Read for homework (4)		Text to self-connections
	Choice to read or not (7)	Book projects (2)		Set purpose for reading (2)
				Scaffolding (4)
				Imaging
				Vocabulary games

Strategies for Building Readers' Confidence

Particular strategies that students believe would build their reading confidence included SSR and choral reading. Sustained silent reading, while a controversial topic regarding the degree to which it supports improved student reading, addresses the same issue students raise about the desire for more classroom time spent in actual reading. They need more time to read the texts required in the classroom.

Choral reading was a strategy of great interest. Choral reading is an oral reading strategy where the teacher and students read the text simultaneously. It can work to build student confidence because those students who have difficulty with oral reading would be supported by the stronger oral readers in the classroom. Choral reading is typically a strategy used for beginning readers, but older readers do read at a variety of levels, so this strategy can still be helpful to students. It can also scaffold English language learners to learn the academic language so necessary for knowledge acquisition.

COMPARING TEACHER AND STUDENT THOUGHT ON ■ READING CONFIDENCE

When comparing the two charts of what teachers and students think about developing reading confidence, similarities and differences emerge. What is most interesting and delightful is that students have a real sense of what they need to become more confident and proficient readers. Additionally, the ideas expressed by both teachers and students are often complementary. If teachers' and students' voices and beliefs can be accommodated in content classrooms, the reading required not only will be less of a struggle but also will increase students' learning self-efficacy.

Figure 2.4 compares the way teachers and students think about what should happen in the everyday learning interactions within classrooms. When asking students to read, the teachers thought more about eliciting verbal input from students whereas students were more concerned about just being able to negotiate the meaning of the required reading. Vocabulary is an area of content teaching not always seen as important by teachers. In this specific comparison, teachers did not address it at all while students see it as the most important aspect of their daily reading.

The differences in terms of curricular approaches that teachers and students feel would develop reading confidence are based on providing choice in materials versus the manner in which students would read. Teachers thought more about choice, while students thought more about issues of safety and time for reading. Both groups recognized the importance of teaching reading strategies for building confidence, and thus teachers might plan more strategy development in their lessons. Students did not necessarily reflect on what they were required to read for school, but felt that whatever they needed to read, they would prefer that their teachers allow them to do so in class, in a safe environment, and be taught strategies for learning how to read the texts required. Teachers thought that more choice would be valuable.

Figure 2.4
Comparison of Teacher
and Student Thought

Teaching and Learning Relationships

Teachers:

1. Sharing and valuing opinions

2. Asking lots of questions

3. Present finished products from reading.

Students:

1. Address/teach vocabulary

2. Rehearsed read-aloud

3. Use texts on instructional level (slightly challenging)

Curriculum Planning for Enhancing Reading Confidence

Teachers:

1. Use of multiple materials

2. Choice

3. Model learning & knowing

Students:

1. Time to read in school

2. Read aloud in safe atmosphere

3. Teach strategies for understanding

Affective Interactions and Confidence

Teachers:

1. Positive comments

2. Know students

3. Value all student input

Students:

1. Motivate by encouragement

2. Rewards

3. Believe in students

Strategies for Building Readers' Confidence

Teachers:

1. Literature circles

2. Retellings

3. Rehearsed oral reading

4. Word walls

Students:

1. Sustained silent reading

2. Choral reading

3. Paired reading

Students and teachers have similar ideas about how the way teachers treat students can help produce reading confidence. While students suggest rewards as a way to build confidence, teachers believe that knowing students and valuing what they have to say are more productive.

Comparing the specific strategies that are suggested by teachers and students, we list the strategies cited most often by each group. When considering both lists, a crucial difference is that while literature circles might be considered similar to paired readings, students want the smaller groups—pairs. To produce confidence, teachers and students may have different processes for developing reading self-efficacy. Students want pairs of readers, choral reading, and silent reading, suggesting safety in their reading development. Teachers believed that literature circles, oral retellings (or summarizations), and rehearsed oral readings would produce confidence.

◼ AN ENVIRONMENT FOR BUILDING READERS' CONFIDENCE

Middle and secondary teachers as well as their students consider classroom environment a critical element that could produce more confident readers. Two major adjectives that recur among teachers are "supportive" and "responsive." Classrooms that are supportive of students' efforts and responsive to students' needs produce more confident readers. Establishing such an environment requires thinking about how content reading is addressed, as well as the common practices that occur within particular content classrooms. Students suggest that classrooms need to become more democratic and collaborative, while also engaging ideas that match teachers' concerns about being supportive and responsive.

Oral reading is used in many classrooms for a variety of purposes. Yet if students do not feel comfortable in their oral reading endeavors, the classroom environment can become a place that is not supportive, and students can feel as though their teachers are not responsive to their individual reading needs or challenges.

The rest of this chapter highlights the multiple ways teachers can create more supportive and responsive classroom environments that promote the development of success and confidence among content readers. Using particular materials, teaching methods, and classroom interactions, teachers can facilitate their students' reading development.

Reading in Content Classrooms

Many content area teachers rely upon the use of the textbook related to the content subject for the most of the required reading. This seems reasonable since the textbook typically covers the knowledge expected to be covered in the content curriculum. There is reason, though, to evaluate the relationship between curriculum guidelines; readers' different reading abilities; and textbook structure, format, content load, and readability. If there is a mismatch within this complex relationship, students may have difficulty comprehending the information they are expected to garner from the text. For instance, readability tests in a variety of middle-level social studies textbooks reveal reading levels that are often higher than the grade level of the audience addressed.

Other textbooks have too dense a content load, particularly for many middle school students. By "content load" we mean how much new information is given in the relatively short space provided in the text for that information. For instance, a science textbook may give the definition of a phenomenon like photosynthesis, the circumstances under which the phenomenon occurs, a variety of examples and nonexamples of the phenomenon, and the causes for which the phenomenon may not occur. This type of information is expected in a textbook, and those who select textbooks for a school or district may specifically look for this type of information when choosing one for their student population. However, it is important to look at the amount of actual space given to covering the phenomenon in a particular chapter or text. If the text gives all the information in a relatively short amount of space, student readers who lack sufficient background knowledge about the content may feel overwhelmed and not be able to absorb all the information. This feeling of being overwhelmed constricts students' feelings of confidence, and they can begin to feel as though they cannot learn the material.

Combining potential mismatches between readers, texts, and curricular mandates with oral reading issues can create a content classroom that is neither supportive nor responsive to students and their needs. Many adolescent students are still working on reading proficiency and comprehension, and oral reading in the best of situations can be intimidating for many of them. If content textbooks contain too much new information, or are written in a format or structure relatively unfamiliar to students, students' oral reading skills may suffer. Once they have attempted to read orally and feel less than adequate about their performance, their confidence can deteriorate and their feelings about their cognitive abilities to even *learn* the material may also suffer. Thus finding ways for students to practice their oral reading that are less intimidating can help them become more proficient not only at oral reading, but also at acquiring the topical knowledge they are expected to learn. In essence, by asking students to read in small groups and to practice their oral reading skills with the content text is a positive step toward building reading confidence and knowledge acquisition in all content areas.

Classroom Practices for Building Reading Proficiency

Returning to the idea of self-efficacy, since confidence resides in the affective domain (students' feelings), but influences cognitive development (the ability to *learn* the information required), teachers need to consider content classroom social cues and environmental situations because particular environmental behaviors and curricular designs can increase student confidence (Sanacore, 2000; Swafford & Bryan, 2000; Williams, 2001). Workshop environments, where affective and cognitive interactions between students and teachers occur more often on a one-to-one basis, develop students' confidence about their reading and learning.

When attempting to provide the support and responsiveness adolescents need to develop their reading confidence, teachers might try talking explicitly with their students about reading. Since confidence is more about attitude and feelings rather than accomplishment, recognizing students' attitudes about reading and accepting their different perspectives on reading creates a more supportive and responsive environment. Working from this foundation, teachers begin building reading interest and engagement through particular curricular decisions and teaching strategies. By engaging in honest dialogue about reading and then creating classroom engagements that support and encourage personal reading development, teachers can provide an environment that supports all types of readers.

Once students gain an understanding about themselves as readers, their confidence can be more fully developed. As Goodman (1996) asserted, "Readers' beliefs about themselves as readers often influence their literacy development." Environmental conditions set the stage for students' beliefs about themselves and their learning. Creating classrooms and learning conditions that foster students' confidence is ultimately under the control of teachers who establish the classroom environment.

■   STRATEGIES FOR BUILDING READERS' CONFIDENCE

The following section provides additional strategies to build reading confidence and proficiency, and extends upon some of the previous suggestions.

Using materials and methods along with assessment strategies that allow students to understand themselves as readers creates the space for increased self-knowledge, which is one of the cornerstones of confidence. Additionally, using class meetings where students may discuss their feelings about reading and the types of reading that interest or challenge them, teachers create an environment of safety that allows adolescents to attempt new behaviors in relation to reading. This risk taking increases their confidence in themselves, which produces a willingness that enhances skill and strategy development.

Class Meetings About Reading

Class meetings are times when the teacher gathers the students together to discuss challenges, questions, or issues that arise in the classroom. During these meetings, teachers invite students to discuss the direction the class is headed, whether that may concern social interactions, cognitive development, or curricular decision making.

In relation to reading confidence, talking with students about their reading preferences, interests, and issues can create a climate where students can become more aware of or comfortable with their abilities. This is not to suggest that students will be forthcoming about the challenges they face with reading, but rather, they will begin to understand that not all readers have the same abilities or appreciate the same types of texts, text structures, or reading interests. The types of reading discussions in Figure 2.5 are good for building confidence in adolescent students.

Figure 2.5
Classroom Meeting Reading Discussions

Classroom Meeting Reading Discussions

Types of Meeting	*Purpose for Meeting*
1. Discussions about reading interests	These meetings allow students to consider their reading interests in relation to the content under study. It also allows students to become aware of the kind of reading they like such as expository, narrative, poetic, and so forth and see the preferences of other students.
2. Discussions about reading challenges	These meetings allow students to discuss where they find the most difficulty in their reading. Through this self-awareness, readers can begin to address their difficulties with the teacher's additional support. This also allows students to recognize that all readers may have difficulties with some aspect or type of reading.
3. Discussions about particular texts	These discussions allow readers to address the reading they had to complete for a particular topic or assignment. Through these kinds of discussions, students can honestly address their feelings and recognize that others may have similar feelings. This creates a zone of safety and comfort for the students while allowing the teacher to recognize the types of texts students may find difficult or boring.
4. Discussions about types of readers	These discussions create an awareness of how students feel about themselves as readers, in both negative and positive terms. Through honest discourse about their reading abilities, students come to understand themselves better while also recognizing that they are not necessarily good or bad students or people.
5. Discussions about reading growth	These discussions become an exercise in self-reflection that allows students to see how much they have grown as readers and how their interests or abilities have changed throughout the year. Again, such meetings are also good assessments for both the students themselves as well as the teacher.

Class meetings about reading throughout the year allow students to reflect upon their reading growth as the year progresses. For most of these meetings, teachers will have to begin by modeling how to talk about reading. Using themselves as models, teachers can show students that every reader has interests, preferences, and challenges. By discussing their own growth as readers, teachers help students understand how readers continue to develop reading proficiency well beyond the elementary years.

The one class meeting we suggest teachers not conduct until second semester and after a comfort level has been reached within the classroom is the "Type of Reader" discussion. This can be an awkward or damaging interaction unless a supportive classroom environment has been established. Those who have difficulty with reading often feel unworthy and thus, the confidence and self-esteem to do well in schools. Poor readers feel unlovable, and while language such as "unlovable" may not seem appropriate for discussions about reading proficiency and learning, it is a very real phenomenon. In a safe and accepting environment, the reason these types of discussions build confidence is that they allow students to become more comfortable with who they are as readers as well as noting that others in the classroom feel like they do. Often adolescents who have difficulty with their reading feel isolated from their peers. These meetings bring young readers together while also allowing the teacher to better understand the types of readers within the classroom and how they may be supported in their reading development.

Using Authentic Texts

Another way to build confidence in adolescent readers is using authentic texts. Authentic texts produce reading events that are similar to the actual reading people perform in the world, not just in classroom situations. Authentic texts are trade books found in bookstores and libraries, and are written for the public, not just for classroom situations or reading instruction. The use of authentic texts or trade books allows young readers, especially those who may be having difficulty with reading already, the opportunity to work with materials they will use once they leave the classroom.

There are multiple ways to provide authentic texts to students. One way is through school and community libraries. Students typically use school libraries where they are allowed to search the Internet and check out books of their choice. Where possible, the local library is also a positive place to find and use authentic texts, while also exposing young people to libraries outside their schools, and the availability of texts for their use outside of classroom situations.

Another way to provide students with authentic texts is through thematic instruction or an inquiry curriculum that requires students to complete research on a topic under study. By working with their school librarian or media specialist, teachers and their students can find texts that address a particular theme. Teachers can collaborate with local libraries on texts for their classrooms. Community libraries often allow teachers to check out a large variety and number of books for classroom use.

The use of authentic texts within the classroom gives adolescents a taste of the types of books and other materials available to them for content studies. Such authentic material makes reading a much more real activity because it allows students to see the variety of texts written about a specific subject, as well as how the content they are learning is relevant to the world outside the classroom. Authentic materials build reading confidence because they are the written in language that students encounter in outside reading. Textbooks are often too ponderous and too overburdened with content facts to create a reading experience that is conducive to aesthetic reading, which is beneficial for reading engagement. (Figure 2.6 explains aesthetic and efferent reading stances.)

Figure 2.6
Aesthetic and Efferent Reading (Rosenblatt, 1938, 1995)

Aesthetic reading is reading that allows a reader to be more fully engaged with the author's world or content. We often say such reading allows the reader to become "lost in the text."

Efferent reading is reading for pulling out knowledge from the text. Textbooks encourage this type of reading, which for many adolescents simply means finding the answers to teacher questions or the questions at the end of a chapter and then forgetting the information after the unit or topic has been covered.

Rosenblatt, who theorized about these two types of reading stances, suggests that readers are frequently utilizing both stances within any reading event, but textbooks and classroom reading too often focus more on efferent reading, which may not develop more interest in reading.

Accessing Prior Knowledge

To help improve reader confidence, it is important to access and assess students' prior knowledge before asking them to read new material. Quite often, students do not possess the background knowledge necessary for them to understand the current reading they are expected to complete. For instance, some students in different parts of the United States have little understanding of geographical features found within their own state, much less other parts of the country. By accessing their prior knowledge, then assessing what they do or do not know, a teacher can first build the prior knowledge needed for a study of different biomes or topological features so that all students have a sense of what they are studying. Showing pictures and videos also allows students to visualize what they are studying.

Another strategy for accessing and assessing students' prior knowledge is through free writes. At the beginning of a unit, teachers can ask their students to free write in journals about the topic to be studied. For instance, when teaching the European Holocaust, the teacher can place the word *Holocaust* on the board and ask students to write what they know about this phenomenon. Knowledge is likely to vary greatly and incorrect information may be revealed. After a ten-minute period, volunteers can share what they have written. From there, the teacher can begin a unit knowing what students already know, what misconceptions they bring, and what interest they exhibit in the topic.

Making Connections to Reading

Along with building students' prior knowledge, it is helpful to ask students to connect what they are reading to their own lives through metaphors or analogies. Zimmermann and Keene (1997) suggested three types of connections:

- *Connecting to the self:* Students can make these connections to their own situations or lives.
- *Connecting to other texts:* These connections are to other texts or materials the student has encountered through reading or viewing.
- *Connecting to the world:* These are connections to world or community events that the reader knows about.

By making connections to their readings, students build their confidence about what they know and what they are reading.

Paired Reading With Peers

As suggested by the students who answered questions about reading self-efficacy, one strategy that could build their confidence is paired reading. Paired reading is a strategy that allows two readers to read—either silently or aloud—the same text, and then to discuss what they have read. Selection of readers can be up to the discretion of the teacher, or students may select their own partners for reading. Paired reading can be accommodated by giving reading time in the classroom (another suggestion listed by students). Reading aloud to another person supplies students with the opportunity to practice their oral reading skills, and the discussion after each page or section of the material read creates a space for students to check their comprehension. If both partners have difficulty with a passage, the teacher can opt to discuss the passage with the twosome, or the whole class, or find another text that addresses the same content but at an easier reading level.

Teachers can model paired reading by creating a "fishbowl" experience that has one student working with the teacher in front of the classroom. The other students observe the interaction, thus creating a "fishbowl." Another strategy to scaffold paired reading is reciprocal teaching. Figure 2.7 explains this strategy. By using this strategy, students begin to see how proficient readers approach the text as well as how they discuss the knowledge they are gaining.

Figure 2.7
Reciprocal Teaching
(Palinscar & Brown, 1986)

Teacher demonstrates strategy:
 1. Teacher selects a passage from the textbook or other piece of expository text.
 2. Teacher begins to read and demonstrates predicting what might happen.
 3. Teacher then generates questions that someone might ask about the passage.
 4. Teacher talks through unknown words or confusing phrases or ideas.
 5. Teacher summarizes what has just been read.

Students then pair up and go through the strategy together:
 1. One partner begins by reading one paragraph.
 2. Partners then predict what they think will happen and why.
 3. The second partner asks the reader questions from the reading.
 4. Partners discuss answers to questions.
 5. Partners select and discuss unknown words and confusing concepts or phrases, being sure to justify their answers.
 6. The reader then summarizes the passage.
 7. Partners switch roles.

Paired Reading With Younger Readers

Similar to paired reading is a strategy of pairing middle school readers with younger students. This would also give the older students time to rehearse their reading, which was suggested by middle school teachers and would benefit students' oral reading performance. This works best if two teachers at different grade levels work together on a similar thematic unit.

The middle school students would help their teacher select appropriate materials for reading aloud to the younger students, practice reading the selection orally, and then be paired with another student from the lower grade. Middle school students who participate in such ventures return to their classroom with a renewed respect for reading aloud, classroom management, and the importance of discussion. Through this type of reading, middle school students also feel connected to and appreciated by the younger children.

Word Walls

Though gaining in attention, vocabulary is one of forgotten elements of content reading. Vocabulary, however, is of critical importance to students. Word walls are often used for elementary students, but are appropriate for middle school and younger secondary students as well. The word wall is a large piece of white or butcher paper that lists the new words students or teachers find related to the content under study. Creating thematic word walls for students helps them recognize how particular words relate to one another, to specific topics, or to content or topic areas. In social studies, thematic word walls might be created for historical, geographic, or economic terms. In science, word walls might be related to the scientific process, biological systems, or other units of study. In language arts, word walls can remind students of poetic language or new words found in their novels. In math, word walls are especially useful for reminding students of mathematical processes and the particular signs used throughout that content area.

Some teachers remove word walls after a unit is complete, but students should be exposed to the content language throughout the year. The teacher can point out words on the word wall whenever the teaching context allows for this. Students need multiple exposures to a word before really assimilating it into their vocabularies. It is valuable to explain to students that they have multiple vocabularies: listening (the largest vocabulary they own), speaking (typically the smallest vocabulary they possess), reading (the second largest vocabulary they have), and writing. Students also possess differing vocabularies depending on their interests and their knowledge of particular topics or content areas. Placing the words on the wall is simply not enough for most students. They need to actively attend to the words placed on the wall. Students can be required to use the words orally and in their writings.

A FUN chart is a place where students can list words under the letters F, U, and N. Figure 2.8 shows how FUN charts work. The letter *f* represents *familiar word*s, which the student has seen or heard but does not really know. The letter *u* stands for *understand*s, which are words the student may understand the meaning of but he or she still needs to work on the spelling or pronunciation. The letter *n* means *new word*s, and the student may have to spend more time learning those words than other words on the chart. Students should be encouraged to add to their FUN charts, but they must also be encouraged to use the words they place there. Writing exercises, discussions around the topic or theme under study, and multiple exposures to a word are all ways to provide the deeper contact and knowledge of required content language.

Figure 2.8
FUN Vocabulary
Charts

Students create a chart like this one in their content notebooks. They then place words they need to work on underneath one of the following letters. If the students know and understand a particular word, there is no reason to place it on the chart.		
F (familiar but not known)	U (understands but cannot spell or pronounce)	N (new words)
asteroid	gyroscope	heliometer

Using Text Sets

Text sets contain a variety of texts on the same topic with multiple reading levels. They also contain texts with differing text structures and formats such as novels, picture books, informational texts, and poetry. Recognizing the importance of using multiple materials, text sets also allow for choice in materials, and they address students' requests for slightly challenging materials that would increase their reading confidence. Selecting text sets can be done with the help of media specialists or bookstore personnel. With the variety of trade books written each year with younger audiences in mind, teachers can find a plethora of texts to use for most units they are expected to teach.

Retrospective Miscue Analysis

We would be remiss if we did not mention retrospective miscue analysis (RMA) for boosting adolescent students' reading confidence. Typically conducted by language arts and reading teachers, or by reading specialists, RMA requires students to orally read a piece of text on their reading or instructional level without the help of the teacher. The session is audio taped and then analyzed by the teacher for the types of miscues observed. After this analysis, the teacher and student meet together to discuss the miscues noted and why the reader may have made those miscues. RMA is an empowering experience for middle school readers because it typically focuses on the strengths the reader brings to the reading event and the belief that miscues are not mistakes, but rather the prior knowledge the reader brings to the text. Developed by Goodman and Marek (1996), and based on Goodman's work in miscue analysis, retrospective miscue analysis is reader centered and created specifically for older readers.

■ CONCLUDING REMARKS

By understanding that confidence is not always about accomplishments or success, we come to realize that students who display confidence are not necessarily the best students, and in fact, may actually shy away from some tasks or challenges. Confidence is not always about doing well or completing a task. It is primarily about self-knowledge and a willingness to take risks outside areas of comfort because students are already comfortable with who they are and what they have been able to do, learn, or accomplish in the past.

Building young readers' confidence is realized when teachers create a positive environment that is safe enough for all those in the community of learners to take risks and try out new behaviors. In such an environment, readers who are quite sure that they cannot read a particular text are encouraged to try. This happens when they realize they really have little to lose because they are supported by the teacher and their peers in the classroom. Further support comes from tasks and strategies that scaffold their reading abilities while also building them. Support also comes from peers and teachers who are willing to let them attempt new reading behaviors without ridicule or embarrassment. Such an environment can be established only once all of the members in the learning community recognize that the diversity in perspective and development that is part of the world they live in is represented in their classroom.

Students cannot build their confidence in reading, however, without also realizing that it is dependent upon opportunities to read and work independently, acquire metacognitive awareness and strategies, and build stamina in relation to the reading tasks placed before them. A reader's self-efficacy is enhanced by developing each one of these elements and utilizing them together to become more proficient at reading and learning. The following chapters will examine how these elements can be fostered.

3

The Importance of Independence for Gaining Reading Proficiency

Teachers recognize that it takes more than students' confidence in their reading skills to create proficient readers. The second aspect of reading self-efficacy is students' ability to negotiate a text independently. In fact, many educators suggest that the primary indicator of reading proficiency for middle and secondary students is their ability to read independently. Independence is a cornerstone of life in our democracy, providing the ability to choose and the opportunity to make decisions about one's happiness. When discussing reading independence, experts suggest that independence is about the ability to choose which strategies help with understanding the reading task as well as the actual way to go about reading.

Independence

Independence is the ability to apply a specific literacy strategy after determining the literacy demands without the aid of another.

Example

This is a hard concept to understand, but I think if I read parts of it aloud, I might understand it better.

Development of student independence is often tied to students' interests and their stance toward the content being read or the task required. Additionally, independence may rely on the strategies that students know, on the strategies teachers stress in reading particular texts, and on ways the environment allows or does not allow students to practice their reading through reading experiences, classroom invitations, and materials that ask students to bring their reading skills to a task.

In this chapter, we discuss what teachers and students say about reading independence and how it can be developed through curricular engagements, reading materials, and classroom interactions.

■ WHAT TEACHERS HAVE TO SAY ABOUT READING INDEPENDENCE

As we have stated in previous chapters, this text is informed by numerous teachers who have worked with secondary students over varying lengths of time. The practices and processes through which they believe independence can be developed or encouraged in middle and secondary school readers appear in Figure 3.1. Again, these ideas are sorted by the five teaching domains identified in Chapter 1. As they did with reading confidence, teachers found ways to increase student independence by addressing environmental issues, explicit strategies, and classroom practices and processes.

Teaching and Learning

Teaching and learning relationships that help develop reader independence include a number of experiences that teachers can implement in any classroom. As the chart in Figure 3.1 shows, there are everyday teaching strategies teachers can either include in their planning or use spontaneously to help build their students' reading proficiency. Two elements teachers find beneficial are providing students with a repertoire of strategies they can use on their own when reading and allowing students to edit their own written work, which helps not only with their reading but also with other literacy skills.

Additionally, teachers recognize the importance of students taking ownership of their work and responsibility for completing it. Of course, students often need teacher scaffolding with some of the more difficult reading or literacy tasks required in their content classrooms. Yet allowing students to begin the task independently and then working with them toward completion not only builds students' reading skills, but also provides opportunities for teachers to work with students who need more help than their peers.

Another aspect of teaching and learning that teachers noted was creating opportunities for students to make personal connections to the content they are learning. So often, teachers feel compelled to complete a topic or unit because of state or district mandates, but if students are encouraged to make connections or create metaphors and analogies to the content they are studying, they are more apt to remember it. And with this remembering, they are more likely to make connections to the next topic under study and to have the ability to read the next section or text independently. For, as we mentioned in Chapter 1, independence is not a natural state; it must be learned. As students learn strategies and skills for comprehending a text, the more able they will be to utilize those skills in subsequent tasks.

Environment	Teaching/ Learning	Curricular Decisions	Affective Decisions	Strategies
Collaborative Transformative Democratic	Providing strategies for reading and writing that students can use on their own (32) Support but not give answers (4) Let student(s) be the teacher (3) Students edit own portfolio (25) Provide ways to organize work (3) Practice with good questioning strategies (4) Provide assignment calendar (3) Encourage ownership of work (6) Opportunities for students to make personal connections (7) Encourage students to question accuracy (2) Encourage use of references	Multilevel scaffolding (4) Utilize zone of proximal development (3) Opportunities to apply learning (2) Text sets/multiple materials (24) Opportunities for students to talk about learning with each other (3) Use of an inquiry approach (40) Application of Bloom's taxonomy (2) Gradual release of responsibility (2) Technology Class meetings (2)	Belief that all children can and do learn (3) All are equal members of the learning community (3) Provide time for decision making and choosing, encourage initiative (6) Value of learning how, not memorize and spit back Students taking responsibility for daily classroom routines Recognizing each student is unique (4) Recognize and promote all learning styles (4)	Sustained silent reading (31) Debate (2) Skimming/scanning appropriately (4) Analysis and synthesis (4) Quick write (3) Think aloud (26) Brainstorming (20) C3B4 Me (3) Note taking (20) Outlining Self-monitoring (12) Use of dictionary, thesaurus, and so forth

Figure 3.1
Independence: Pedagogical Factors Reported by Teachers (N = 107)

Curriculum Planning for Enhancing Reading Independence

The comments teachers made about enhancing students' reading independence show that many of them believe they should be creating curriculum that gives students a variety of materials to use as well as text sets (mentioned in Chapter 2 as well) that can scaffold students' reading proficiency. The use of texts on differing reading levels helps students gain proficiency while also helping them acquire the content. By using text sets, students can read a variety of texts on the same topic, which again helps them understand the topic in more depth and serves as a way to scaffold their reading abilities from easier texts to more difficult.

While the use of multiple materials was a large factor in the teachers' thinking, the most frequently cited curricular factor was the use of an inquiry approach to learning. By using an inquiry curriculum, teachers both address the foundational knowledge they feel students should know and allow their students to investigate the questions about that content that seems most interesting to them. For instance, if students are required to know about the U.S. Civil War, teachers plan to teach the general knowledge required by the mandated curriculum. They also, however, allow students to pose their own questions about aspects of the Civil War that seem especially interesting to them. Questions may center on the role of women during the Civil War, Civil War heroes, Civil War prisons, or a particular battle or event. With an inquiry curriculum, students take ownership of their own questions and the process for finding the answers to those questions. This increases their reading and research independence.

Affective Interactions and Independence

The third category of teacher response to our interest in students' reading efficacy involved the interpersonal relationships within the classroom setting. Examining Figure 3.1, we noticed that teachers realize that independence does not just exist but is produced with the help of others. Students' reading independence needs to be encouraged by teachers through small steps that might include allowing students to learn in multiple ways, encouraging students to take the initiative on some class projects, and allowing students to help with the curricular planning. Additionally, teachers believed that if students know their teachers feel that all students can learn and that all students are equal members of the learning community, students would be encouraged to become more willing participants in classroom learning, regardless of the content area.

Strategies for Building Readers' Independence

Teachers listed a number of strategies to help students become more independent readers. These included brainstorming, think-alouds, note taking, and SSR. Other strategies mentioned included asking students to self-monitor (which will be discussed in Chapter 4) while reading, skimming and scanning appropriately, performing quick-writes, and using other comprehension skills such as analysis and synthesis. Learning how to use these skills depends, however, on teachers taking the time to teach these strategies, especially in relation to the specific materials often utilized in each particular content area.

Teachers desire to improve their students' reading independence as well as their reading confidence, but are often deterred from teaching reading processes because of time constraints and content topics to be covered.

■ WHAT STUDENTS HAVE TO SAY ABOUT READING INDEPENDENCE

Using the same categories mentioned previously, we also plotted on a separate matrix students' beliefs about what would enhance their reading independence (as seen in Figure 3.2).

Teaching and Learning

In middle and secondary schools, students are still learning how to take control of their own lives and actions. They still have difficulty taking responsibility for their own learning, regardless of how many years of practice they have had with homework and classroom projects. Thus, they still need their teachers' help with reading and learning how to negotiate the demands of all types of texts independently. Students reported that they want their teachers to teach them reading strategies and to help them with their reading. The students also reported that they need time, with no disruptions, to practice their reading through SSR.

Environment	Teaching/ Learning	Curricular Decisions	Affective Decisions	Strategies
	Discuss books	Time for SSR (98)	Encouragement/ praise (16)	Books on tape (2)
	Conferencing with teacher (8)	Fewer time limits/due dates (25)	Motivate with rewards (18)	Read-alouds (8)
	No disruptions in sustained silent reading (15)	Choice and variety of books (66)	Given time to do it before interrupted (8)	Paired reading (3)
		Recommendations (29)		Visuals (TV)
	Teach strategies (40)	Limited interruptions of SSR for projects and programs (AR, work book questions, group work, tests) (58)		Rereading (2)
	Give students time to figure out reading problems (8)			Questioning (2)
	Tutoring (5)			Sustained silent reading (98)
Comfortable	Goal setting	Reading for homework (8)		
	Allow for own pace	Battle of the books		
	Discuss importance of reading			
Respectful	Help us with reading (15)			
	Read aloud to us (5)			
	Solicit parent help (2)			

Figure 3.2
Independence: Pedagogical Factors Reported by Students (N = 270)

Curriculum and Reading Independence

One of the most important elements that came from student reporting is the need for SSR time. Approximately one-third of all the students with whom we worked requested that they be given time to read; thus, teachers need to plan for that time in their curriculums. Another large factor reported by students was the opportunity to choose the materials they wish to read, and for teachers to have a wide variety of reading materials available. Therefore, when planning curricula, teachers will need to find a variety of materials that address similar content so students can select texts that are engaging to them while also presenting the information teachers want their students to learn.

Figure 3.3
Selecting Texts for Reading Choice (Major criteria for text selection in content classrooms)

1. Reading Abilities of Students: Accommodating all readers in a classroom means finding texts that they can read on their independent level and instructional level. Teachers can find books on a variety of topics and at all levels by using picture books, informational texts, and chapter books. This also helps with scaffolding readers as they become more independent.
2. Reading Interests of Students: Finding books on subtopics under a larger concept or area of study allows students to address particular interests they may have in relation to the topic under study. Finding a wide variety of texts also addresses the variety of students' desires as well as collecting resources for an inquiry curriculum.
3. Expanding the Classroom Library: Selecting texts that expand the topic and the subcategories under a larger concept allows for greater variety. Finding texts that are narrative, poetic, and expository also allows for comparisons of text structure.
4. Accuracy and Authenticity of Texts: Texts need to be selected according to their accuracy and authenticity. Accuracy concerns facts, while authenticity addresses the realness of the text. Does it reflect real details and real ways in which people lived and spoke? There can be times when a text gives factual information but lacks authenticity because the way the facts are presented does not actually depict the reality of the topic.
5. Multiple Perspectives on a Topic: Selecting texts that present different perspectives on the same topic allows readers to develop their critical literacy skills in relation to author purpose and stance as well as accuracy and authenticity.

Affective Interactions and Independence

Interesting enough, students had little to report in the way of affective interactions in the classroom. Some students reported that they needed praise or encouragement while others asked to be motivated through rewards. In the overall information shared by students, very few actually mentioned any affective measures needed to be taken. Perhaps the idea of reading independence means that students believe they need to be intrinsically motivated, and not rely upon teacher incentives or attitudes.

Reading Strategies to Enhance Independence

Another interesting result from the information reported by students was the lack of particular strategies they felt they needed to become independent readers. We find, however, that their request for strategies along with the lack of being able to articulate any specific strategy reinforce the notion that students need to be explicitly taught strategies that will help them become more proficient readers. Some of the strategies students did name, however, included read-alouds by the teacher, and SSR. Again, the need for time and strategies comes across loud and clear in the students' responses to our questions about reading independence.

■ COMPARING TEACHER AND STUDENT RESPONSES TO READING INDEPENDENCE

A quick look at how students and teachers think about reading independence and classroom procedures and practices allows us to see the similarities and differences between the two groups. Figure 3.4 presents information in relation to the categories we discussed previously.

Figure 3.4
Comparison of Teacher and Student Thought on Reading Independence

Teaching and Learning Relationships	
Teachers:	Students:
1. Provide reading strategies	1. Teach strategies
2. Edit own portfolio	2. Help with reading
3. Allow students to make personal connections to content	3. No disruptions of SSR time

Curriculum Planning for Enhancing Reading Confidence	
Teachers:	Students:
1. Use of inquiry	1. Time to read in school
2. Multiple materials/text sets	2. Choice and variety of reading material
	3. Projects and programs for reading

Affective Interactions and Confidence	
Teachers:	Students:
1. Encourage students	1. Motivate by encouragement
2. Recognize student uniqueness	2. Rewards
3. Value student input	

Strategies for Building Readers' Confidence	
Teachers:	Students:
1. Sustained silent reading	1. Sustained silent reading
2. Teacher think-alouds	2. Teacher read-alouds
3. Note taking and brainstorming	3. Paired reading

Teachers and students both recognize the importance of strategic reading and knowing strategies to become strategic readers. The disconnection between students and teachers occurs with the disruption of SSR time. Students reported that they are interrupted during silent reading time, yet this might be the time when teachers ask students to make personal connections to the materials the students are reading.

Another divergence between student and teacher reporting was the importance of reading portfolios. Many teachers felt reading independence could be developed by allowing students to maintain and edit their own reading portfolios. Students did not mention portfolios at all, suggesting that this practice in schools, especially in relation to literacy and student independence, might need to be reconsidered. Another possibility might be that students do not see how the work on their portfolios involves independence.

There were differences in terms of curricular approaches that teachers and students felt would develop reading independence, yet these differences seemed to only be in terms of the language used. Students mentioned the use of reading projects, while teachers suggested an inquiry approach to learning would be beneficial to students' reading independence. Since inquiries typically produce a project that involves the need for reading, we find that the teachers and students have similar ideas about what can produce independent readers and learners. Additionally, both groups mentioned the need for multiple materials. The teachers added text sets, which can simply mean more texts of the same title so that more students have access to particular books or media. Students mentioned the need for variety, which would allow them to read about the same topic from multiple perspectives. Overall the only difference we were able to ascertain between students and teachers was the students' request for more time to read in school.

Students and teachers have somewhat different ideas about what affective measures are important for reading independence. In sheer numbers alone, the teachers had more ways in which they felt they could value their students and the work their students do in class. Students, on the other hand, had little to say about how teachers might treat them or interact with them to produce more reading independence.

Comparing the specific strategies that were suggested by teachers and students, both groups believed SSR would help produce more independent readers. Interestingly, the teachers' input about think-alouds is comparable to the students' desire for teacher read-alouds. Both groups can be accommodated by blending these two strategies.

When considering both lists, the information known by teachers versus what is articulated by students becomes a crucial difference. Students lack the names of strategies or, perhaps, even the ways in which they can become readers that are more independent outside of SSR. Teaching strategies explicitly might narrow this gap.

Overall, the patterns of student thought center on two large categories: (1) time to read independently and (2) choice and variety in reading materials. Teachers acknowledged the need to teach students more reading strategies and to allow for more choice and variety in reading materials. Additionally, the teachers noted that an inquiry curriculum would also produce readers who are more independent. We find that allowing students to learn through an inquiry curriculum would accommodate both the time for reading and their request for choice in reading materials.

■ AN ENVIRONMENT FOR DEVELOPING READING INDEPENDENCE

Historically, independence is built from a foundation of freedom, choice, and opportunity and is necessary for creating independent readers. Literacy proponents also address motivation (Gambrell, 1996; Tovani & Losh, 2003) and fluency (Worthy & Broaddus, 2002) as markers of reading independence. If these characteristics are signs of reading independence, then classrooms need to be encourage, develop, and maintain these elements. Teachers have the privilege and the opportunity to create environments that allow for such conditions and practices.

Classroom Conditions That Create Reading Independence

According to our review of the studies about reading independence, the opportunities afforded by the classroom environment are an important aspect of producing proficient readers. The teachers and students with whom we worked suggested that the classroom needs to be comfortable, collaborative, and respectful of differences. Additionally, the teachers suggested that a democratic classroom where students' opinions are expected and respected can transform the way teachers and students go about learning. A transformative classroom can create enthusiasm and active learning that engages students beyond the classroom to more active involvement in their neighborhoods and communities. In relation to reading independence, transformative action means students take what they have learned from classroom materials and apply that knowledge to the wider world in which they live.

The issue of collaboration needs to be noted when discussing the production of independent readers. We find that students become more willing to work independently on aspects of a project when they feel they have a responsibility to other students. One way for teachers to create collaborative classrooms where independence is encouraged is through real-world projects that allow students to contribute their own unique ideas to a plan that will take a group to complete, for instance, having students think about ways to improve their neighborhoods. One group of sixth graders with whom we worked thought their neighborhood needed more trees. Thus they wrote letters to businesses and civic organizations for contributions, read about which trees grow best in their climate, and studied what was needed for trees to take root and grow. Individual students were responsible for their part of this real-world activity, but the entire project was a collaborative effort. Group activities that require students to have responsibility over their own part of a project allow them to be independent and collaborative. The only danger is when too much responsibility is placed on a student at one time. By watching students closely, teachers can quickly discover who needs help on any part of a project. This issue brings to mind how important teachers are when attempting to facilitate students' growth toward reading independence. Through scaffolding, teachers can create greater and greater reading independence in their students.

Scaffolding Reading Independence

Independence is often procured by scaffolding students as they learn to negotiate more difficult texts, writing genres, or different text structures and formats. Through methods and models that gradually release responsibility (Pearson & Gallagher, 1983) to students, teachers facilitate the move to their students' independent literacy usage and production. Thus teachers will want to establish a collaborative classroom environment where the teacher makes students feel comfortable with the required reading and learning.

Working toward reading independence while also making students feel comfortable can be time-consuming, yet well worth the time. By working with students in small groups, in one-on-one tutoring sessions, or by simply using word walls with basic procedural and conceptual information displayed, teachers scaffold learning. An additional way to scaffold is through a constant dialectic of teaching and assessing knowledge so that a teacher knows when to support students more and when to release the responsibility of their reading and learning to them. Overall, by noting when students may need more or less teacher support, or when they need to be left to their own reading or reminded to use any number of reading strategies, teachers help develop more independent readers.

STRATEGIES FOR CREATING READING INDEPENDENCE ■

Teachers can use numerous strategies to help their students develop reading independence. The particular strategies we highlight here can readily be scaffolded for student use, thus allowing all students to progress toward reading proficiency.

Interest Inventories

While the use of interest inventories seems almost common sense, we suggest that they are seldom used in content classrooms. What do students enjoy in terms of science and social studies content? In what ways do they see how their lives are conditioned by mathematical processes and concepts? How do historical events produce current situations? In what ways does geography play a part in culture, diet, and politics? When we asked students about the basic conceptualizations of some of their content studies, many could not tell us what the social studies were. They did not connect history to the present; they did not understand how frequently they used mathematical concepts to negotiate their daily lives. They seldom connected their own curiosities about the world to the content they were learning in their secondary classrooms. Yet such connections could easily be made from simple interest inventories taken at the beginning of the year or a topical unit. By finding analogies and subjects related to the content under study, the teacher can bridge the content to be covered in class to student interest. By creating analogies and bridges to their content areas, teachers not only address student interest, but also begin to contextualize the content studied, and expand the purpose for knowing the mandated curriculum.

Interest inventories can be created as statements related to the content, related content, similar concepts, or analogies that contain similar principles as those the teacher wishes to cover. A Likert scale allows respondents to rate the extent of their interest to the statements provided, usually on a scale of one to five. Students mark their interest from none at all (one) to very interested (five). From the information gathered, the teacher can create an introduction to the content that addresses those interests, drawing the parallels to the subtopics or related concepts that students are interested in pursuing.

Silent Reading

From the information we collected from teachers and students, we know that silent reading is the most important activity for students to do in order to become independent readers. Yet it takes more than just allowing students to read for long periods. We have all watched classrooms where students are supposed to be engaged in an SSR time, only to see individuals staring at one page and others writing notes to one another or completing homework for another class. Part of the importance of silent reading is that students are also allowed to choose their reading materials at that time.

When students receive DEAR (drop everything and read) or SSR time, only to be saddled with required reading, the purpose of that time may be misunderstood. This brings us to the purpose of silent reading. If the purpose of silent reading is to create more engaged and independent readers, then we must allow students to read what interests them. This is not a license to read inappropriate material, but rather a time to select something worth reading and that has value to the individual. Often, however, students are not sure about what is available to them, which brings up the additional element necessary to create independent readers—variety in the materials available. Classroom libraries can fulfill a lot of students' interests, if the teacher takes an interest inventory at the beginning of the year, where the key goal is to find out what students want to read when given time to do so.

Additionally, if teachers know what students like, they can find books or other materials that will feed that interest. This is especially crucial when a student asks for a recommendation. We've built classroom libraries through small school district grants, through work with libraries, and through requests for a small budget to buy classroom texts each year. We have also negotiated the purchase of textbooks with building principals or district coordinators. Instead of buying one book for every student, we would buy half the number and use the rest of the budget to buy appropriate trade books from local bookstores that address the topics we were to study throughout the year.

Questioning the Author

Questioning the author is a strategy that develops students' critical thinking and critical literacy skills (Freedman & Johnson, 2004). Critical thinking skills include those of analysis and evaluation along with differentiating between fact and opinion, while critical literacy skills are those that question perspective; author stance; message, and along with the author's generalization, which is the author's general message about the world or how people live, and so forth (Wilhelm, Baker, & Dube, 2001). Both critical thinking and critical literacy skills are used by proficient readers, yet critical literacy skills are infrequently used with younger adolescents, especially those who struggle with reading. Yet we would argue that all readers need the skills that would help them in differentiating between differing perspectives while also asking about author stance and purpose.

Asking students to question the author is a way of allowing students to understand that texts represent people, ideologies, and ways of being, and that these beliefs and ideas should be supported with facts or accurate details. This strategy in many ways allows students the freedom to disagree with the author's generalizations, but not at the expense of accuracy, authenticity, or truth. This strategy creates a space for readers to think deeply about what is being presented in the text and requires them to think about how they feel about it. We use the following questions when using the questioning the author strategy:

- What do you think the author/text is trying to say?
- What kind of words does the author use to convey the text's message?
- What is clearly explained or not so clearly explained and why do you think this happened?
- What is missing from the text in relation to what it says about the topic?
- What does the author assume that you already know or believe?
- How does the author support the text's message?
- What sources does the author use to support the text's message?
- Are those sources reliable? How would we know?

By using these questions and others, secondary students learn that they can question the message of a text, and they can actually disagree with an author or his or her message. Disagreement, however, must be done with reliable supporting information. Encouraging students to question the author, the author's message, or the author's use of language to present a message are powerful tools that allow students to become more and more independent.

Student Think-Alouds

Teachers use think-alouds to model their reading process for their students. Through a think-aloud, the teacher discusses comprehension, vocabulary, text structure, and stance to the text while also making predictions, asking questions, and making connections. Utilizing think-alouds with students is very similar. We want students to use this process to develop their reading proficiency and independence. The way to do this is by asking a student to think aloud on audiotape while reading a passage from the required reading. Typically, we find a quiet corner to do this so that the student can feel comfortable going through the process. After the student has completed a think-aloud on a short passage, the student and teacher sit down together and discuss what was happening while the student read. This is an excellent way for the teacher to make explicit what happens during the reading process while also enlightening the student to his or her own thinking.

We also like to use this strategy with the entire class. Asking for student volunteers who feel comfortable with the process, we follow the same procedure, but then complete the student-teacher conference in front of the class. The only change is that we ask the audience to become participants in the discussion about the volunteer's reading process by hypothesizing why the reader made specific connections, asked particular questions, or made those predictions. The class can also discuss the particular vocabulary words the volunteer highlighted or stumbled over in one sentence or another.

By completing a think-aloud together as a class, students begin to think about the cueing systems and dimensions of language we discussed in Chapter 1. Being able to use the vocabulary of the reading process is a skill that increases student confidence with their reading because they begin to have control over where they do and do not have problems. This control is also an element of independence and metacognitive ability (which will be discussed in Chapter 4).

Note Taking

Note taking is a skill that is developed with practice over time. It involves the ability to find key concepts, the main idea, and important details. Adolescent readers often need help developing their note-taking skills. Teachers can scaffold such development through interactive note taking. Figure 3.5 explains the concept of interactive note taking.

As the teacher releases more and more responsibility for this exercise to the students, she can also add longer and more complex reading selections for students to negotiate. Once students become adept at selecting main points, the teacher then models how to find supporting details to the main points so students will also learn how important it is to know the context of particular events, the effect of particular processes, or the reasons for particular phenomenon. This strategy can also be done with oral presentations. The teacher can use a prerecorded audio or video speech and then proceed through the recording by pausing every few minutes and asking students what should be noted and what may not have to be written. Teaching students how to chunk information with brief notes can also be accomplished through this exercise.

Figure 3.5
Interactive Note Taking

1. Teacher and students read a preselected section of their textbook or other content material.
2. On an overhead or document projector, the teacher writes a title identifying the selection read.
3. Teacher asks students to volunteer the first main point or key idea they encountered in the text.
4. Teacher asks students to volunteer reasons this might be the first note they should take from the selection.
5. Teacher volunteers reasons for agreeing or disagreeing with students' choice.
6. Teacher then asks for a student volunteer to lead the discussion and write the next note on the overhead, following the same procedure with the class.
7. To further support this process, the teacher again takes the lead.
8. After the teacher's second turn, another student takes the teacher's place.
9. This turn taking continues until the teacher feels comfortable with the students' abilities to find main points and justify their answers.

Other note-taking strategies might include the use of graphic organizers that the teacher can create to scaffold students' learning and eventual ease of use when asked to take notes from an oral presentation. Additionally, teaching students the particular language many speakers use for ease of understanding can also be very beneficial for students' note-taking development and abilities. Words such as *first, finally, subsequently,* and *then* are often used to differentiate time or main points. Again, the utilization of prerecorded audio or video speeches can be used to help students deconstruct the speech pattern used. Teachers can also give their own lectures and use a graphic organizer to show their lecture pattern, or they can use any number of outline structures and fill these forms when talking about content they want to share with the class that is not readily available in the text the students have read.

Skimming, Scanning, and Browsing

These three strategies are related in respect to their use for finding information. When we want to find the answers to questions about a topic or concept, we skim or scan a text for the answer. We do not read the entire chapter or book when searching for an answer to a particular question. Furthermore, when we want to find books on a particular topic, we browse the library shelves or the area in the bookstore that seems most appropriate.

It is the same with our students. When we ask students to find answers to key questions or to define concepts, we expect they can find those answers by consulting the appropriate book, chapter, or passage in a text. Students, however, often do not know how to browse, skim, or scan a text, or if they do, some feel it is cheating. Unfortunately, this feeling can create a sense of drudgery about the assignment resulting in a loss of interest.

One way we ask students to think about finding answers to their questions is by teaching them text structure. By understanding how texts are structured, students are better equipped to search for answers independently. We frequently ask students to do informational book reports, but not ones where they only summarize the text and discuss their responses to it. We should ask them to discuss the format of the text, the figures in the text, and to comment on the additional aids within the text such as the glossary, the index, and the table of contents. By asking students to do this type of book report, where the structure of the text is as important to address as its content, students learn the value of the additional aids the text has to offer.

Another exercise we like to ask students to complete is categorizing texts based on the table of contents and format of the text. We gather a large set of texts that may fall under a larger umbrella concept and then place approximately ten books on tables across the room. We then ask pairs of students to work through the tables, starting with one table and categorizing those books or other materials based on their own criteria. Student pairs move from table to table, adding additional criteria, expanding their category, or collapsing one category into another. The teacher facilitates this learning by working with the pairs as needed.

Through this exercise, a number of objectives are accomplished. The first is that students learn about skimming, scanning, and browsing. The second objective is that students learn how to analyze and categorize texts, a skill often used by proficient readers and learners. Third, students are supporting each other as they become increasingly independent.

Becoming an independent reader requires all types of strategy usage and skills knowledge. By teaching these strategies directly, teachers are facilitating their secondary students' progress toward that goal.

■ CONCLUDING REMARKS

Ultimately, we want adolescents to become proficient, independent readers who are motivated to read, and who can read fluently. To become such readers, many need the help of a teacher, who can scaffold students' learning and reading while developing proficiency. Once students gain a bit of independence, they become more confident, and with this confidence, they are more willing to take risks and attempt more and more challenging tasks. Independence is developed with the help of others who are more capable, but to become truly independent, younger readers also need to be able to monitor their reading as they are proceeding through a text. Thus metacognitive ability is vital to reading independence. Chapter 4 addresses this crucial skill and how it can be developed.

4

A Closer Look at Metacognition and Its Role in Reading Proficiency

Metacognition functions like radar, helping readers detect problem passages and be aware of what they are reading. Students with metacognitive awareness know that a text should make sense and when it does not, they need to make choices and act upon those choices. Metacognitive awareness is crucial in monitoring one's personal reading strategies as well as the reading process. Just as radar can locate objects and render their measurements, a reader should detect a difficult place in the text (object) and account for (measure) this piece of text using strategies that work when comprehension has broken down. In this way, metacognition acts as radar, helping readers navigate through problematic places in the text.

Metacognition is included in C-I-M-S as a self-efficacy element because it involves knowledge of self—self as reader, self as a thinking being, and self as decision maker, choosing which strategy or process to employ while reading a text. Metacognition is the self thinking about what is known and not known, and how the self is situated in this knowing context.

Metacognition

Metacognition is the "awareness and knowledge of one's mental processes such that one can monitor, regulate, and direct [oneself] to a desired end; self-mediation" (Harris & Hodges, 1995, p. 153).

In this way, metacognition constitutes knowledge of ourselves, the kinds of (literacy) tasks we engage in, and the strategies we use while engaged in these tasks (Baker & Brown, 1984; Garner, 1994).

■ WHAT TEACHERS HAVE TO SAY ABOUT METACOGNITION

Teachers have a direct impact on their students' metacognitive processes and skills, because metacognition can develop through teaching and applying specific strategies. Teachers in our study indicated several strategies they shared with their students. Figure 4.1 reports how they develop metacognitive awareness in their classrooms. Again, what teachers shared are sorted into our five domains: (1) environment, (2) teaching and learning, (3) curriculum planning, (4) affective decisions, and (5) specific strategies.

Figure 4.1
Metacognition: Pedagogical Factors Reported by Teachers (N = 107)

Environment	Teaching/ Learning	Curricular Decisions	Affective Decisions	Strategies
Authentic	Plan-do-review	Student-led parent conferences	Support self-correction strategies (6)	Wandering and wondering (3)
Transformative	Discuss how process becomes product (4)	Wide and rich range of reading materials (8)	There are no stupid questions (3)	Use of graphic organizers (23)
	Encourage use of prior knowledge to interpret information (3)	Revisiting the big picture (2)	Recognizing that errors are part of learning (5)	Procedural
	Thinking and questioning (20)	Opportunities to connect the known with the unknown (4)	Pointing out a useful strategy that student used appropriately (7)	Self-talk (5)
	Multiple draft assignments (17)	Options on assignments (4)	Reinforce learning strategies with use of warm-ups (5)	Adjusting rate (7)
	Lots of trial and error (2)	Joint purpose setting and interest generating (5)	Set rules/routines for peer evaluations (5)	Rereading (4)
	Share how answers are found or problems are solved (6)	Opportunities to apply new understandings and knowledge (3)	Model encouraging language and posture (2)	Say it like the character (2)
	Teaching of integrated strategies versus isolated skills (6)	Use multiple sign systems (3)	Feedback reinforces self-monitoring (6)	Induced imagery (15)
	Lots of "why" and "what do you think?" questions (5)	Opportunities to reflect on own and peer work (23)		Context clues
	Use of and understanding the need for the revision process (2)			Self-monitoring (7)
	Use of mutually created rubrics (31)			Explain reasoning when solving a problem (27)
				SQ3R (3)
				Use mental tool belt (5)

Environment

Teachers who report that their classrooms promote metacognitive awareness have transformative classrooms in which they engage in cooperative learning by using authentic texts. Teachers see their role in developing a transformative environment which attempts to help students become aware of reading by providing them with opportunities to read, make judgments about texts, think critically, and generate their own "knowing." Given this environment, teachers then set out to plan for the teaching/learning of metacognitive awareness by making curricular and affective decisions leading to teaching metacognitive awareness through specific strategies.

Teaching and Learning

Clearly, teachers' planning for teaching and learning is at the heart of developing metacognitive awareness in their students. Teachers must plan instruction that provides choices for each student's learning to take place. Teachers voiced that integrated instruction versus isolated skills assured success for each student. The restrictive manner of teacher-directed skills instruction unfortunately allows students to see reading as teacher oriented and not learner centered. Integrating instruction embeds metacognitive processes in real reading and provides students with opportunities for choice and authentic reading experiences. With an integrated approach to instruction, reciprocal peer teaching, questioning, and discussing flourish and metacognition develops.

Reciprocal teaching and questioning places teachers in the role of a decreased emphasis on explicit instruction, thereby allowing students to share with fellow students and teachers as collaborating sources, truly a teaching and learning dynamic. In this kind of classroom, teachers attempt to raise the comprehension bar by having students engage in sophisticated questioning and answering after modeling and sharing the "teaching spotlight" with students.

Curriculum Planning to Foster Metacognitive Awareness

Teachers viewed reflection as paramount in their curriculum decisions. Having students reflect on both their and their peers' work puts the learner at the center of thinking about what they have read. Interestingly, teachers' views of all curricular decisions regarding metacognitive awareness are learner centered. By asking students to think about what they read in different ways, teachers can foster students' reflections on what they have read and help to make them aware that what they think gives them control over how they comprehend text.

Teachers reported curricular decisions which gave students a varied range of reading materials. They realized that when students are engaged in what they read, any reading strategy or activity can be embedded and taught with success. By including authentic nonfiction, fiction, graphic novels, magazines, newspapers, and computer selections in a classroom, teachers communicate to students that reading is for, about, and accessible to them. Choice, in turn, gives students ownership of their reading and understanding of what they read. Metacognition is all about the self and understanding the self as a reader as well as understanding what is read.

Affective Decisions and Metacognition

Teachers are important in their students' lives, and the words they choose and the affect they employ in the classroom are crucial to students' learning. Teachers indicated the following affective decisions as conducive to nurturing metacognitive awareness: (1) supporting self-correction strategies, (2) pointing out when students use an appropriate strategy, and (3) providing feedback reinforcing self-monitoring. Teachers realize the importance of validating their students for attempts to self-regulate and monitor their reading and count these affective decisions as directly tied to their students' success in developing metacognitive awareness.

Strategies to Build Metacognition

For specific strategies which lead students to metacognitive awareness, teachers reported that using graphic organizers, inducing imagery, and explaining reasoning behind solving a problem comprised the list of leading strategies. Teachers also acknowledged that instruction in self-monitoring, adjusting reading rate, and rereading served students well in metacognitive processes.

■ WHAT STUDENTS HAVE TO SAY ABOUT METACOGNITION AND READING

Although metacognition is considered a late-developing skill (Grifith & Ruan, as cited in Israel, Block, Bauseman, & Kinucan-Welsch, 2005), the middle school students in our study had a sense of "knowing" as well as knowing themselves as readers. They reported specific details about what metacognitive awareness is, how it works, and what teachers can do to help them develop metacognitive awareness. In Figure 4.2, students' responses are sorted into the five categories. Students appear to view what should be done to help them gain a sense of metacognitive processes differently than the teachers.

Environment

Students, who are constantly developing metacognitive awareness at this age, determined that an environment conducive to this development called for a responsive, technologically wired, and comfortable setting. Students are quite computer savvy and view the use of computers (wired) as crucial in their literacy development. The call for computer literacies should clearly indicate to teachers that students are well into computer literacy and see the need for instruction in and exposure to this medium to further their computer literacy.

It is not surprising that students indicated a need for a comfortable and responsive environment; humans thrive in positive settings that respond to their needs. Teachers' affective decision making matched quite well with students' need for positive feedback in a setting dealing with understanding themselves as readers.

Teaching and Learning Relationships

Students were very clear as to what they need, and what they respond to, in a teaching/learning dynamic. Students list the following teaching/learning principles that they want from their teachers:

- be aware of their needs
- make instruction explicit
- provide more information through modeling
- perform read-alouds (by teachers)
- offer help with vocabulary
- discuss and reflect on readings
- give more practice time in class

Environment	Teaching/ Learning	Curricular Decisions	Affective Decisions	Strategies
Comfortable	Be aware of needs and point out miscues/errors (15)	Choice in reading (37)	Provide extrinsic rewards (9)	Paired reading (6)
Wired		More time to read (10)		ReQuest (16)
Responsive	Make instruction explicit (24)	Provide viewing and audio (plays, tapes, videos) (5)	Encourage me (6)	Think-aloud (12)
	Provide more information/modeling (21)		Nothing (5)	Note taking (10)
		Small groups (2)	Independence	Connecting (10)
	Help me to think by myself (6)	Read at own pace (2)	Build my desire to read (1)	Viewing/pictures (7)
	More practice in class (16)	Make challenging tests (2)	Support me	Fix-it strategies (4)
		Limit daily required reading		Summarizing (4)
	Help me make choices (3)			Reading logs/ journals (4)
	Independent/uninterrupted practice (10)			Sustained silent reading (3)
	Make it interesting (2)			"So what?" factor (2)
	Help with vocabulary (12)			Literature circles
	Discuss/reflect on the readings (12)			Retelling
	Teacher reads book aloud (17)			"Bell work"
				Imagery
				Book talks

Figure 4.2
Metacognition Pedagogical Factors Reported by Students (N = 299)

Curricular Decisions

Students were very clear about choice of reading material, and choice is a thread running through all four self-efficacy elements. Teachers clearly need to listen to students' pleas for choice. Additionally, students are asking for more viewing as a part of their literacy. This age student is a generation of viewers; videos, plays, and movies are the media they are most familiar with. Teachers are losing out on opportunities with our adolescents by not taking advantage of the many and varied computer literacies as a meaningful medium through which students can apply metacognitive processes.

Affective Decisions

Students want and need encouragement, however; in their youthful desires, they listed extrinsic rewards as something teachers could provide. Extrinsic rewards may have become a way that students view reading rewards today because of the chain stores and American corporations rewarding students for reading a number of books with tangible, edible rewards. Reading rewards may be so closely tied with past practices that extrinsic payoffs are the norm. Encouragement, support, and validation have always been the affects to which learners have responded positively.

Strategies

Metacognition, unlike the other self-efficacy elements, has a number of validated, tested, and researched strategies that have been proven to work well with students. Students specifically delineated ReQuest, think-alouds, paired reading, note taking, connecting, viewing/pictures, and fix-it strategies as the leading metacognitive processes they needed and saw as helpful in their comprehending and thinking about what they read. Although students did not necessarily use the terms indicated previously, they described the kind of strategy or activity that these processes accomplish.

Students in our C-I-M-S study demonstrated examples of the classic research and literature on metacognition. Flavell's (1979) classic article on metacognition delineates a distinction between *metacognitive knowledge* and *metacognitive experiences.* In this distinction, Flavell explained the interaction of metacognitive knowledge and experiences with goals (or tasks) and actions (or strategies). Flavell posited the following variables involving people's held beliefs and knowledge regarding metacognition as *person, tasks,* and *strategies.* For example, if students are working on an inquiry project on the topic, which they have read from numerous texts, of weather and its effects (task), they know that a pie chart and a bar graph are going to give them a lot of information. Therefore, they know that they have to learn to "read" pie charts and bar graphs (strategy) and will go to their friends who can read charts and graphs (person, strategy) for help. This entire process combines person, tasks, and strategies.

Metacognitive knowledge, as it relates to reading, has been organized into three subcategories: *procedural, conditional,* and *declarative knowledge* (Jacobs & Paris, 1987; Paris, Lipson, & Wixon, 1983). Procedural knowledge is an awareness of the process necessary to complete a strategy or task. This involves a student knowing *how* to use context, *how* to discern main ideas from details, or *how* to sequence events for chronology. Students have procedural knowledge if they know about specific strategies, can select the appropriate one, and know how to employ it. Conditional knowledge involves readers knowing "*why* strategies are effective, *when* they should be applied, and *when* they are appropriate" (Jacobs & Paris, 1987). Declarative knowledge involves the three aspects of metacognitive knowledge introduced earlier in Flavell's (1979) work: person, tasks, and strategies. This knowledge focuses on readers' beliefs and on what they know about the characteristics of the text, the reading task, themselves as learners, and possible strategies that can be employed.

Students in this study knew strategies (e.g., think-alouds and fix-it strategies), and indicated that they needed teachers to offer them a choice of strategies and that they wanted to know how to use them. While they demonstrated an awareness of what they needed and what they did not know, they evidently have not developed an awareness with which they are comfortable.

■ COMPARING TEACHER AND STUDENT RESPONSES TO METACOGNITION

Comparing the two charts of what teachers and students think about developing metacognitive abilities shows us the similarities and differences between the two groups. What is most interesting is the students' knowledge of actual strategies they can use to become more metacognitive while reading. This suggests that teachers are addressing self-monitoring and that students have a real sense of what they need to become more capable readers.

Figure 4.3 compares the teachers' and students' suggestions for improving students' metacognitive abilities. When asking students to read during everyday classroom interactions, the teachers suggested using rubrics and coursework that would allow students to "rethink" rather than simply turn in assignments that might be forgotten once they leave the students' backpacks. Additionally, teachers recommended that classroom processes where students had more time to think and question would also help with metacognitive development. Interestingly, student thought complemented much of what the teachers suggested. Student response included more direct instruction with time to practice self-monitoring during class. Furthermore, they desired more teacher modeling through direct instruction or through teacher read-aloud.

The suggestions for curricular approaches that teachers and students feel would develop students' metacognitive skills complemented one another. Teachers recognized the importance of having students reflect, while students thought more about time for reading. Such a cycle of reading and reflecting on their reading allows students to bolster their reading proficiency. Additionally, both groups believed that students should have the opportunity to select reading choices from a wide range of materials. Again, allowing choice but also introducing students to new genres and reading formats would develop students' metacognition but would need to be scaffolded through teacher modeling.

Teaching and Learning Relationships

Teachers:
1. Use of mutually created rubrics
2. Thinking and questioning processes
3. Multiple draft assignments

Students:
1. Make instruction explicit
2. Teacher reads aloud
3. Provide more information/modeling
4. More practice in class

Curriculum Planning for Enhancing Reading Confidence

Teachers:
1. Opportunities to reflect on own and peer work
2. Wide range of reading materials

Students:
1. Choice in reading
2. More time to read

Affective Interactions and Confidence

Teachers:
1. Pointing out strategy when used appropriately
2. Support self-correction strategies
3. Give feedback that reinforces self monitoring

Students:
1. Motivate by encouragement
2. Rewards

Strategies for Building Readers' Confidence

Teachers:
1. Explain reasoning when solving a problem
2. Use of graphic organizers.
3. Induced imagery

Students:
1. ReQuest
2. Think-alouds
3. Connecting
4. Note taking

Figure 4.3
Comparison of Teacher and Student Thought

Students and teachers have differing ideas about affect in the classroom. Students mentioned encouragement without specifics as well as external rewards. Teachers mentioned the ways they perhaps do encourage their students, which suggests that the thinking of both groups dovetails. While students suggest rewards as a way to build students' abilities, teachers believe that addressing specific ways to increase students' metacognitive behavior through the recognition of that behavior is the best way to produce more effective readers.

Comparing the specific strategies that are suggested by teachers and students, we see that students mentioned specific strategies such as ReQuest and think-alouds, while the teachers used more general language for this category. In creating readers who monitor their comprehension of a text, both the teachers and students report similar processes for developing reading self-efficacy. Students mentioned think-alouds while the teacher also used the concept without the specific language. This only tells us that students might assume that we would know the strategies they are learning in schools, while the teachers might not make such an assumption.

Overall, students and teachers have similar ideas about metacognition, its importance to reading self-efficacy, and the practices that scaffold students' abilities to self-monitor. Adding the teacher list to the student list creates far more choices and presents a greater opportunity for growth and development in metacognitive awareness. This further indicates that students do have a sense of what they need, and an awareness of how their thinking and understanding should be accomplished.

■ CREATING MORE STRATEGIC READERS

Two confounding aspects impact teaching metacognitive strategies with middle school students. First, expository texts are the stuff of content teaching. Historically and traditionally, elementary students have not been exposed to expository texts and teachers have more frequently used narrative text to teach comprehension strategies. When students reach middle and high school the development of metacognitive readers is complicated by reading expository texts, the mainstay of middle and high school subjects. Second, teaching strategies for comprehension and/or metacognition have traditionally involved teaching each skill as a stand-alone skill in a somewhat isolated manner—isolating one skill from another. Unfortunately, with single-skill instruction, there has not been a transfer or application to further reading. However, Baker (2001) conducted a study which indicated that adults could manage and apply three processes simultaneously after they had received explicit instruction monitoring propositional, structural, and information completeness. Therefore, we propose teaching multiple metacognitive processes and strategies to help students based on a study conducted by Cummins, Stewart, and Block (as cited in Israel, Block, Bauserman, & Kinnucan-Welsch, 2005). Cummins et al. reasoned that because reading comprehension is not an isolated process activated after reading but rather is a "network of in-the-head processes that work together before, during, and after reading" their goal was "to teach metacognitive processes that would work together to bring about meaning at various times during a reading" (as cited in Israel, Block, Bauserman, & Kinnucan-Welsch, 2005, p. 279).

Therefore, we are combining think-alouds, predictions, visualization and imagery, questioning the author, making connections (to self, text, and world), and self-monitoring as a network of metacognitive strategies. All metacognitive processes involve choice—choices that readers need to make for a text to make sense. The following strategies will allow students choice. Baumann, Jones, and Siefert-Kessell (1993) offered such choices through their think-aloud lessons in which students are taught through verbal explanation, teacher modeling, guided practice, and independent practice.

Block and Israel (2004) acknowledged that educators have asked for more information about how to perform effective think-alouds that are highly effective in promoting metacognitive awareness. Block (2004) asserted that metacognitive awareness significantly increases students' self-assessment of comprehension while honing students' abilities to select strategies to overcome text difficulties while they read. Block and Israel (2004) also indicated that struggling readers are most in need of think-alouds as a metacognitive awareness strategy and listed twelve effective ways to accomplish think-alouds. Metacognition allows for confidence, independence, and stamina.

Think-alouds are always modeled by the teacher who reads aloud a passage while thinking out loud as to what is involved in the thought processes going through the teacher's mind:

- "This word looks like another word I know. I'll try this definition to see it if it works."
- "This character reminds me of Billy in the last story I read."
- "This process is like the process for making a lever and pulley."
- "I predict the next action will be…because…"
- "The word *messy* brings a picture to my mind of how my daughter's room looks."

In this way, the teacher allows the student to think about other thoughts connected to the reading of a passage:

- Create a picture
- Make a prediction
- Try a definition for a new word
- Make a connection to personal experience (self), to another text read, and to prior knowledge of some outside event

After this, students can be paired with a reading partner to share their thinking and then read on to see if their thoughts are realized.

Imagery and *visualization* are terms we use for students being able to "make movies in their head" or create visual representations that help them understand texts. Image making can begin with wordless picture books, allowing students to view how artists, illustrators, and authors make concepts understood through pictures. Students can gather several pictures from these sources and "write" a story with using only pictures. As they share their stories through pictures, the class can then be placed into groups of two or three and write stories using words. These words and pictures are then student-created media of how words are pictures and pictures are words. Then students can read descriptive passages and share the pictures in their minds with each other. Marshall (2001) also suggested "art practice" strategies in which students transform what has been experienced or observed into images (p. 88). Marshall described such a practice for idle school students in which they can cut out pictures from old history texts and make collages to tell their own version of history.

Another instructional strategy that has students interacting with, thinking about, and questioning while reading is question the author (QtA). Devised by Beck, McKeown, Hamilton, and Kucan (1997), this strategy has students "talking with the author" and questioning the author about a text. The teacher is crucial in modeling the strategy by

- selecting a text and reading the text closely with students;
- identifying major passages that cause problems; and
- creating questions to be asked at certain points prompting students to think about what the author suggests by rereading text.

These questions need to validate how the author is communicating the intended message. This process should be continued throughout the text.

QtA is especially important in building metacognitive awareness because it explains an important metacognitive principle to readers. If a reader does not comprehend what the author is attempting to communicate, it may not be the fault of the reader. This clearly places the onus on the student to be metacognitive in making sense of the text/author.

Self-monitoring is really what metacognition is all about. Opitz and Rasinski (1998) have a student self-evaluation monitoring organizer that could be made into bookmarks for all students to keep for narrative reading that prompts metacognitive processes. In Figure 4.4, students can have a ready reminder of what and how to fix things when reading narratives.

Students have several metacognitive strategies that can be theirs; the key is the teacher. Metacognitive students need metacognitive teachers.

Figure 4.4
Student Self-
Evaluation

Student Self-Evaluation

Name _____ Date _____
Title of book _____
Pages read _____

Directions
  1. Read each statement.
  2. Check the appropriate column.

I understood what I read.
I tried to sound just like the character so other could understand how the character was feeling.
I read smoothly so that my voice would sound just like it does when I talk with a friend.
I read just right—not too fast and not too slow.
I knew when I was running into trouble, and here is what I did:

_____
_____
_____
_____
_____
_____

ARE WE PREPARING METACOGNITIVE TEACHERS? ■

Unfortunately, the teachers and students in our study often displayed areas of differences between what teachers said they did and what students perceived teachers as having done. Metacognitive teachers are reflective practitioners. As such, they are what most teacher education programs attempt to develop and to have enter the classroom. Reflective practitioners seek to solve problems through inquiry about practical situations. The inquirer shapes experiences by continually probing for better ways to solve problems within given situations of practice (Schon, 1983). Reflective practitioners are metacognitive thinkers and doers, thereby preparing students to become metacognitive readers. The question then becomes one of teacher development: Are teachers prepared in such a way that fosters, develops, and promotes metacognitive teaching and thinking?

Teaching is fraught with difficult decisions often made instantaneously in a profession riddled with uncertainty. Duffy (as cited in Israel et al., 2005) claimed that visioning is the essence of metacognitive teaching, going on to define it as "[imposing] control over one's work, especially given the pressures teachers face today, one must have a strong sense of personal mission" (p. 302). Duffy went on to state that although visioning is his term, Bandura labeled it "self-efficacy" (p. 302).

Duffy (as cited in Israel et al., 2005) stated that experts in teacher education need to focus on four goals, resulting in major shifts in teacher development: (1) teachers should foster a mental model in which they are "in charge," (2) teachers should become leaders of their professional development with experts as coaches supporting them, (3) experts in curricular decisions should help teachers develop abilities that transform knowledge not just to "know," and (4) teacher preparation experts should serve time on-site "to ensure that teacher learning occurs in the context of the real classrooms" with expert assistance provided (pp. 304–306).

Duffy (as cited in Israel et al., 2005) presented a strong case for preparing metacognitive teachers; it calls for a change in the traditional teacher-education paradigm by having teachers take charge and make decisions in collaboration with teacher educators. These goals mirror what good metacognitive teaching calls for with K–12 students—exert oneself in one's learning and bring oneself to reading.

Clearly, today's literacy programs with scripted lessons, prompted by results of timed literacy assessments that label students with little or no application to instruction, do not reflect metacognitive teaching and learning.

CONCLUDING REMARKS ■

Metacognition, coined by Flavell in 1979, has opened a whole body of research on teaching, thinking, and awareness of self as reader and thinker. Metacognitive awareness is crucial to effective teaching and learning, and leads to a reader's independence. Students and teachers with authority over their learning and teaching possess the self-regulatory know-how to comprehend text and know themselves as learners. If knowledge is power, then the access to power is through knowing oneself and knowing how to learn. Metacognition may be the strongest of all self-efficacy elements as it helps one develop the confidence, independence, and stamina needed to pursue knowing. And metacognitive students are the results of metacognitive teachers.

5

The Significance of Stamina in Reading Proficiency

The self-efficacy element of stamina becomes a crucial factor when a learner is not willing or able to complete an extended literacy engagement. Our definition of stamina is closely connected with a reader's confidence, independence, and metacognition. However, while stamina builds from the other three efficacy elements, it also supports them because the stamina that readers have enables them to willingly and ably journey through uncharted terrain in pursuit of a learning goal when interest and purpose are the driving forces.

While stamina is mentioned in the research as a necessary ingredient in the literacy process of proficient readers, there has not been a great deal of work that looks at just what stamina is and how it works. As discussed

---

Stamina

Stamina is the learner's ability to persevere and pace herself or himself when a literacy engagement becomes difficult or lasts longer than expected. It is "sustained reading, sustained writing, sustained discussing without direct and continuous prompting from the teacher or peers, self-regulation of time use, ability to organize time" (Freedman, Thomas, & Johnson, 2003).

---

in Chapter 1, related studies have focused on such concepts as continuous engagement. Au (1997) indicated that ownership and self-confidence result in focused engagement, which in turn creates stamina. Berliner and Biddle (1995) and Tobin (1984) asserted that learners engage in literacy tasks based on the concept of on-task behavior, which we have found to be a result of stamina rather than an impetus for it.

Other concepts that can be associated with stamina include the significance of the nonvisual (F. Smith, 2004; Kucer, 2005) information a reader brings to a reading event; that is, background knowledge, purpose, and interest. Stamina is dependent upon background, interest, and purpose, as the goal of reading is to make meaningful connections between what one knows and what one is learning. M. Smith and Wilhelm's (2004) work based on Csikszentmihalyi's (1990) idea of flow is another associated concept as it is through a sense of competence that readers are willing to continue to pursue information and ideas. They suggested that "developing students' interest and competence before they are given a challenging assignment is crucial" (p. 460).

In a study of sixty-six striving readers, Fink (2006) discussed the "trait of persistence—the ability to bounce back after failure" as an ingredient that helped these readers develop "resilient attitudes and habits, try new solutions and accommodations and ultimately develop their talents" (p. 96). Essential to this development of persistence was the concept of interest, which provided purpose. "Interest is a generative force for all kinds of learning, especially learning to read" (p. 136).

Santa (2006) used the term *active persistence* in connection with the idea that learning requires effort and engagement. She suggested that active persistence can be developed through teachers getting to know their students' backgrounds and interests and creating relevant purposes for reading and learning.

■ WHAT TEACHERS HAVE TO SAY ABOUT STAMINA AND READING

As in the previous chapters, the voices of over one hundred teachers appear in Figure 5.1 sorted into four of the five teaching domains identified in Chapter 1. The environmental domain that pertains to stamina incorporates the importance of seeing learning as continuous, incremental, and developmental. These three foci demand that the learning environment incorporate many of the items listed in Figure 5.1, as discussed later.

Teaching and Learning

The teachers felt that the most important aspects of the teaching and learning relationship involved the direct engagement of students in the work of the classroom. For example, negotiating rubrics for assignments and facilitating student planning become critical elements in building stamina. Developing and sustaining the abilities to self-monitor classwork and to plan for each day and from day to day become major components in perseverance and persistence. Much of the teaching and learning relationship also demands that the teacher model these aspects of stamina and plan for ways to whet student appetites for reading, writing, and talking.

One way to do this is by initiating a specific reading or reading about a particular concept, topic, or theme and then leaving students to finish the specific reading or choose from materials offered in a text set on the concept, topic, or theme.

Environment	Teaching/ Learning	Curricular Decisions	Affective Decisions	Strategies	
Continuous Incremental Developmental	Negotiate rubric allows students to monitor selves (25)	Allow plenty of time to explore and choose (3)	Allow students to stand or walk while reading (3)	Create project timelines (9)	**Figure 5.1** Stamina: Pedagogical Factors Reported by Teachers
	Read half the reading; have students finish it	Provide multiple ways to do an activity (10)	Provide minibreaks (5)	Use chunking (5)	
	Plan sequential activities (5)	Plan pacing (2)	Allow water bottles	Keep dialogue journals (25)	
	Increase length for each activity by a few minutes each time (5)	Use read-alouds (40)	Encourage good nutrition (3)	Help students maintain a sustained discussion	
	Provide lots of sharing time	Use contracts and criteria for the contracts (2)	Avoid too much teacher monitoring (5)	Plan sustained silent reading (25)	
	Long-term projects (4)	Put agenda on board each day	Provide climate of success (4)	Plan sustained silent writing (2)	
	Visual representations of progress (3)	Provide choices (4)	Plan your way out of a job	Plan for a long-term project (3)	
	Introduce projects in steps (4)	Include high-interest print and activity (4)	Reinforce student responsibility for task completion (4)	Discus process with peers (6)	
	Model sticking with something	Sustained silent reading regularly in each content area	Facilitate organization	Ask questions (3)	
	Facilitate student planning (2)	Connect pleasure reading with content reading	Show interest by listening (2)		
	Whet appetites for what is next		Be aware of body language and signals (3)		
	List daily objectives for longer projects (4)				

Curricular Decisions That Enhance Reading Stamina

In thinking about curricular decisions that will influence stamina development, teachers need to consider three major ideas: the role of choice, the role of deliberately assessing and building necessary background, and the role of sustained periods of time for students to read and write alone or to discuss and collaborate.

Choice is a major factor is learning. Negotiating engagements while keeping the curricular goals at the forefront is the key to increased stamina. Students need to be an integral part of deciding what is to be done, in what time period, and with what result. Teachers provide choices from among several preplanned items or allow for students to actually brainstorm options, depending again on the learning goals and the unit of study. Choices can range from choice of print materials to choice of project focus and assessment tools used for the student to demonstrate their learning.

Using experiences, wide reading, and discussion to build the background that the reader needs to access the information in the print materials is an ongoing and recursive process. Often teacher read-alouds work well here to initiate student sharing of experiences both in their lives and with print materials of similar content. From here, students are interested enough and have sufficient connections with the content to delve back into the print materials provided and engage in SSR. Just as useful for this purpose are some of the rehearsed oral-reading strategies such as Reader's Theatre (Opitz & Rasinski, 1998), in which students plan and perform for the interest, engagement, and edification of their peers as well as themselves. This coupled with the Say Something Strategy (Short, Harste, & Burke, 1996) to initiate discussion can be a powerful way to build student stamina.

It is also essential to provide time for learners to reflect, consider, and connect with the materials they are reading. Using learning logs, draft books, and journals is an excellent way of accomplishing this. Two examples of formats that can be easily used follow in Figures 5.2 and 5.3.

Figure 5.2
Reflection Journal (Freedman & Johnson, 2004, p. 232)

Name _____ Date _____
Topic:
Brief summary of topic:
How this topic affects me, my community, and the world:
Negatives and positives about topic and process:

Figure 5.3
Dialogue Journal Entry (Freedman & Johnson, 2004, p. 235)

Name _____ Date _____
Discussion topic:
Discussion partner:
Key points of the discussion:

Affective Decisions and Stamina

The affective domain involves developing a climate of success, clear rights and responsibilities of the learners, and readily accessible organizational tools. For example, students need to know that their teacher not only expects them to succeed but will give them all the support they need to succeed. This trust is built around negotiated rights and responsibilities generated by the learning-centered classroom community. Regularly scheduled class meetings can be a major key to the success of developing these relationships between teachers and students and students and students.

It is also important to support students in their organizational strategies. Disorganization is confusing, and it is too easy to let not knowing where to begin, where the materials are, or what book was used yesterday give a learner an excuse to give up. Providing students with guidelines and support to regularly maintain a portfolio or notebook is another key to the student persevering even when there appears to be stumbling blocks. A place for each student to refer to see what was done before and to have kept the things that need to be accomplished next is essential.

■ WHAT STUDENTS HAVE TO SAY ABOUT STAMINA AND READING

The students' responses as can be seen in Figure 5.4 mirror in many ways the responses of the teachers. The environmental domain described by the students used the words *comfort, flexible,* and *organized* to describe the optimum environment for developing and using stamina to maintain the flow of academic learning. The emphasis, however, is different. The students focused to a great extent on extended time for reading and being able to choose the reading. The students were also more specific about certain aspects of reading for which they felt they needed support such as learning vocabulary, choosing appropriate print materials, finding encouragement, and dealing with challenge.

Environment	Teaching/ Learning	Curricular Decisions	Affective Decisions	Strategies
Continuous Incremental Developmental	Provide practice (10) Goal setting (8) Help with choices (8) Help with vocabulary (7) Explicit instruction (8) Individual attention (5) Do not tell words (2) Discuss reading (2)	More reading time (43) More time limits (6) Choice in reading (64) More reading (45) Scaffold easy to hard (14) Recommend good books (11) Oral reading (8) Reading homework (2) Challenging books (3) Structured programs Author studies	Encourage me (22) External motivation (13) Challenge/push (5) Never quit (4) Energy Concentration Being prepared Desire Enjoyment Discipline	Games (7) Read-alouds (5) Pronunciation (3) Speed reading (5) Sticky notes Answer questions Self-correction Books on tape Choral reading

Figure 5.4
Stamina: Pedagogical Factors Reported by Students

Teaching and Learning

Two things that differed from the teachers' responses included the students' request for more class time to read within the context of print materials of their choosing. This differs from traditional SSR programs including Accelerated Reader in that the reader's interest and purpose are connected to the learning within science, social studies, math, health, and other units of study. For example, choosing texts from a text set of multiple materials within the study of biomes would allow students to select appropriate materials for themselves based on the purposes negotiated within the unit, background brought by the student to the content, and interest developed by frontloading activities (Wilhelm, Baker, & Dube, 2001). When given twenty or thirty minutes two or three times a week, students can make tremendous strides not only in stamina development but also in content learning.

Students also requested more vocabulary development. One strategy for this that works well in tandem with word walls (discussed in Chapter 2) is for each student to keep a personal glossary in their portfolio or notebook. This personal glossary consists of words or phrases that the student is encountering that he feels he needs to know in order to comprehend the content. These can be organized in different ways depending on the needs of the student. They can be organized by alphabet, by concept, by print material, and so forth.

Curricular Decisions That Enhance Reading Stamina

The students agreed with the teachers that time and choice were essential to building stamina. They went even further, though, in their emphasis on the role of challenge in helping them to build stamina. The students voiced the idea that teachers need to walk that fine line between challenge and support. This is where students' taking responsibility to request assistance when needed becomes a key component in teacher planning. Teachers must provide a mechanism that affords students the opportunity to push forward knowing that if they hit the proverbial wall and they cannot work through it themselves, they have a classroom procedure for getting help either from the teacher or from a peer.

Another strategy that allows students to meet challenges is to provide all students in the class access to common texts, such as novels, articles, and so forth—materials that everyone will need to have comprehended. Using books on tape (or CD) is an excellent way to provide everyone with access to the shared information and ideas. From this shared reading, students develop the interest and purpose to go into materials that are appropriate for them within any particular unit of study.

Affective Decisions and Stamina

In the affective arena, students echoed the teachers' goals, expressing the need for the teachers to encourage the desire to learn. As mentioned in the teachers' section previously, it is imperative that teachers take the time to know their students well enough to create appropriate frontloading (Wilhelm, 2001) activities such as wandering and wondering among a text set of multiple materials and generating a list of questions as well as a list of concepts they are familiar with, completing an experiment, or inviting a guest speaker to talk with the class, and so forth. Through these kinds of engagements, students build the necessary desire to maintain and broaden their stamina.

■ COMPARING TEACHER AND STUDENT THOUGHT ON STAMINA

Comparing what teachers and students thought about developing reading stamina, we found both similarities and differences between the two groups. We found the category of curricular decisions to be the most interesting because of the differences expressed by teachers and students. These differences, especially when noting how many students suggested that they wanted choice in reading as a way to build their reading stamina, are compelling.

Figure 5.4, a comparison of teacher and student thought about reading stamina suggests that there are multiple ways to help students become more proficient readers. When asking students to read in everyday classroom interactions, the teachers suggested the use of rubrics that would allow students to know in advance what was expected of them. We believe this may be a way of allowing students to work incrementally toward a goal in manageable units rather than simply turning in assignments at a particular time. Additionally, teachers recommended that sequencing of activities might also allow students to build their reading stamina. Student responses included the need for more practice, help with their choices, and goal setting. When thinking about the ways the students spoke about reading stamina, we recognize that they believe with practice their development as readers will increase. Additionally, being given manageable goals allows them to pace themselves, yet they also ask for help with some of their choices, further suggesting that they need to be scaffolded in terms of what they are reading and perhaps the time they are given for a particular reading assignment.

Teachers, when asked about curricular planning, thought that using read-alouds would help with student stamina. We believe this could help with stamina because students could develop their listening skills, their pacing for reading, and also build their interest in the content the teacher may be addressing in the read-aloud. Interest, understanding how reading is done by those who are proficient, and hearing text language in their heads can discipline students' reading habits in terms of mental energy. Once disciplined, they are better able to put that discipline to work with independent reading. Students complement this thinking by asserting that they need more choice in their reading (interest), more classroom reading (types of texts), and more reading time (utilizing their mental energy to develop their own stamina). We see in these answers to our question about building reading stamina two groups from different sides of the classroom dynamic essentially saying that it takes time, practice, and interest to build stamina.

When examining how students and teachers talked about affective decisions that might produce stamina, we found that teachers recognize that students need breaks. If we agree that students' mental energy is utilized when they are reading, then they also need periods of time to rest from that activity. Many proficient readers find themselves taking breaks from their reading through pauses, note taking, or simply rethinking what they have read. Young people often need to take more physical breaks. A fifth grader with whom we worked said the best way she read was "to read a little, play a little, and then do it again." Teachers also mentioned trying to avoid too much teacher monitoring. Time on task is a different concept than stamina, and often we find that if students take the breaks they may need as they read that they are not on task. Perhaps that thinking needs to be reexamined in light of building students' reading stamina.

Students requested encouragement and external rewards as ways to build their stamina. We are not convinced that rewarding students with candy or prizes will produce stamina, but we are certain that students appreciate when their teachers notice their attempts to improve, and such appreciation can result in more focused attempts at developing their reading stamina and proficiency.

Comparing the specific strategies that are suggested by teachers and students, we noted that students mentioned games, read-alouds, and speed-reading. Games can improve student interest in reading, while speed-reading may be another way to think about skimming and scanning, which addresses a reader's purpose for reading. Students may feel that their stamina can be increased by knowing how to skim and scan, and we agree. Students may find that they will spend longer on a reading activity if they are not struggling with too many pages or too dense a reading load. This can be especially true for middle school students who are still learning how to read more complex content materials. Teachers mentioned strategies like dialogue journals and SSR. Allowing for time meets the needs for students to work in increments, decide when to take the break they may need, and to find something of interest that will engage them during SSR time. Dialogue journaling also gives students the break they may need while also addressing their desire to share their interests with another reader. By making reading an engaging activity that addresses their interests, teachers can produce opportunities for their students to develop their reading stamina.

Overall, students and teachers recognized the value of developing reading stamina as a way to create more proficient readers at the secondary level. Developing the wherewithal to continue on a demanding task is essential for all students as they progress through school.

■ AN ENVIRONMENT FOR BUILDING READERS' STAMINA

While the teachers and students chose different words to describe a positive learning environment, their words mirror each other. For a learning environment to be continuous (teachers), it must be comfortable (students). For learning to continue incrementally (teachers), the environment must be flexible (students). And for the environment to provide for developmental growth (teachers), the work of the classroom must be organized (students). The students are keenly aware of what makes learning accessible and doable for them. Each of these descriptions of learning-centered classrooms provide for the continuous development of stamina.

■ STRATEGIES FOR BUILDING READERS' STAMINA

The major implications for teachers and for teacher educators in creating reading stamina are threefold. The first is to create learning experiences that provide literacy engagements in which their students will be successful and as such will build confidence and a sense of competence. The second is to provide students with ample opportunities to choose from among multiple materials those pieces that they find interesting and to which they bring sufficient background and purpose. The third centers on the importance of teachers getting to know their students well and promoting relationships within their classroom learning communities. These would include relationships between the teacher and each student and between and among the learners, and those that go beyond the classroom to others in the school and the wider community. For example, both school and community librarians can be excellent partners in supporting and promoting reading stamina. In Figure 5.5, we offer a composite of the suggestions made by the students and teachers in our study for specific actions taken within classrooms to support and create stamina.

It is interesting to note how similarly the teachers and the students recognized the key elements in building reading stamina. The most essential ingredient that all of their suggestions point to is the creation of fully functioning, democratic classroom learning communities where everyone is a full participant with negotiated rights and responsibilities.

Opportunities for Success	Choices & Multiple Materials	Development of Relationships
Representations of progress	Provide choices	Flexibility
Praise initiative	High-interest reading materials	Awareness of body language and signals of students
Praise for finishing a project	Providing multiple ways to do an activity	Show interest by listening
Planning sequential activities	Long-term projects	Use of contracts and clear criteria
Point out how much has been done, how long students have been reading or who much they have written	Use of trade books and other print materials	Connect with students interest
Increase the length of time for an activity by a few minutes each day	Choice other than textbook	Encourage good nutrition
Calendars/useful pacing	Read for a certain amount of time not number of pages	Provide minibreaks as needed
Provide a climate for success	Use of dialog journals to initiate sustained discussion	Whet appetites for the new
Provide time lines to follow	Allow students to stand or walk around while reading	Model expectations and strategies, that is, think-alouds
Skip what you do not know and go back later if needed	Acts of inquiry to increase Interest and purpose	Use teacher read-alouds
Landmarks for long projects	Maintaining interest and Involvement	Assist with student planning for long-term projects
List daily objectives for long projects	Allow plenty of time to explore and choose something to read	Teacher must be tuned into each student
Encourage organization	Opportunities to control the use of class time	Provide lots of sharing time
Negotiated grade rubric to help students monitor selves on how they use their time		
Put agenda on the board daily		
Feeling comfortable to learn and grow from wherever they begin		

Figure 5.5
Building Stamina in Learning-Centered Classrooms

Support Strategies

Specific strategies that provide support for students to meet with success include using graphic organizers, completing daily planners, posting projects as well as daily agendas with important due dates, and scaffolding silent reading.

Graphic Organizers

Graphic organizers are an excellent way to keep students' momentum active by allowing them to see their progress in developing content understanding through reading and writing (Johnson & Freedman, 2005). Such graphic organizers as concept maps, concept feature analyses, and know/familiar with/new (KFN) charts are delineated in Figure 5.6.

Categorization of Information

In this strategy, students list the items that they are reading about that demand analysis. They then list all of the ways in which they need to analyze each item. Students create a grid with the items that all fall into the same category listed vertically and the ways each will be analyzed listed horizontally (see Figure 5.7).

Knowledge Charts

Knowledge charts offer students the ability to deliberately make use of what they already know and the background they bring to the reading and learning. A knowledge chart requires that students use three columns to list things they know, things that are familiar, and things that are new. The middle column is the one that is most important as many times students think they know more than they do. They confuse having a passing recognition of a word or an idea with a real understanding. This chart then helps them see that while they have a lot to build on, they still need to attend to details and dig deeper for more information. Figure 5.8 is a knowledge chart about the solar system.

Figure 5.6
Graphic Organizers

Concept Maps

Concept maps are visual representations of how the main ideas and details of a concept, topic, or theme can be organized. These maps demonstrate the relationships between and among the main ideas and details. Using a concept map, a student can answer such questions as: What is it? What is it like? What are some examples?

Analogy Graphic

Using an analogy graphic, a student can compare two concepts by listing their similarities, differences, and categories.

Different Perspectives Outline

Using a different perspectives outline, a student selects a position and a perspective other than the book's. The student maps out needs, concerns, text statements, and reader reactions to text statements and provides a summary position statement from the perspective selected.

Discussion Web

Using the discussion web, a student starts with a yes or no question, then lists reasons for yes or no answers, and develops conclusions based on those reasons, which allows for discussion of the validity of the reasons and conclusions regardless of a yes-or-no belief answer.

Frayer Model

Using the Frayer model, a student defines a concept by listing essential characteristics, nonessential characteristics, examples, and nonexamples.

History Change Frame

Using the history change frame, a student shows in a flow chart how people's actions can either solve or create problems, the changes that occurred because of the actions, and the effects of the problems or solutions on people.

Mind Mapping

Using a mind map, a student demonstrates new information by defining it and then giving broad characteristics.

Pyramid Diagram

Using a pyramid diagram, a student starts with a topic or concept, then builds information about the topic in layers, becoming increasingly detailed.

Semantic Map

Using a semantic map, a student starts with a central concept in the middle of the page and then connects concepts or content extending out from the center.

Story Map

Using a story map, a student addresses who, what, when, where, why, and how and gives information about the theme or intent of the text for discussing the information.

Structured Note Taking

Using structured note taking, a student addresses text structure and how information is presented in a text (Buehl, 2001, as cited in Johnson & Freedman, 2005, pp. 87–88).

	Size	Distance from the Sun	Number of moons	Physical makeup and atmosphere	Distance from Earth
Mars					
Mercury					
Venus					
Neptune					
Saturn					
Uranus					
Jupiter					
Earth					

Figure 5.7
Planets

Things I know	Things that are familiar	Things that are new
There are eight planets.	Most planets have moons.	Saturn's rings are made of rocks and ice.
Mars has waters and is red.	Planets go around the sun.	Earth has an atmosphere.
	An atmosphere means gas.	Other planets' have atmospheres.

Figure 5.8
KFN Chart

Choice Strategies

Specific strategies for providing choices and multiple materials involve wandering and wondering, practicing question asking and problem posing, and providing multiple assessment possibilities for students to use to demonstrate learning.

Wandering and Wondering

Within the study of a content topic, students who have access to a selection of multiple print materials are more likely to engage in wide and sustained reading. Getting students engaged with the texts involves initial browsing and sampling of the materials by wandering through the books and as they do so, initiating questions the print and pictures make them think about. The wandering part involves "looking at the pictures and other graphics, reading captions, stopping to read sections of text that grab their attention, and informally sharing the information and their connections with it" (Freedman & Johnson, 2004, p. 45). The wondering part involves posing questions and problems suggested by the browsing. As students' curiosity is piqued, they almost automatically begin to ask questions and wonder aloud a number of "what ifs." It is the recursive nature of finding information, connecting with it, and then wanting to know more that strongly supports the development of stamina. This happens without students even recognizing it as it is such a natural learning process. Figure 5.9 is a sheet that supports the work of wandering and wondering.

Assessment Strategies

The chart in Figure 5.10 offers suggestions of assessment strategies that allow students to show their learning in authentic ways that provide ample opportunities for achieving success and feeling a sense of accomplishment. This in turn promotes students' perseverance into uncharted territory.

Figure 5.9
Wandering and
Wondering

Name _____ Date _____

Title and author:

Pages:

1. Item of interest:
   Information:
   Connection:
   Questions/problems:

2. Item of interest:
   Information:
   Connection:
   Questions/problems:

Title and author:

Pages:

1. Item of interest:
   Information:
   Connection:
   Questions/problems:

2. Item of interest:
   Information:
   Connection:
   Questions/problems:

Figure 5.10
Assessment Strategies
(Freedman & Johnson,
2004, pp. 168–169)

Predict: silent readings, uses of context, uses of prior knowledge, quick writes, exit cards, experiments

Solve: journals, interviews, dialogue journals, debates, experiments, uses of analogies and metaphors

Discover: silent reading, browsing, skimming, scanning, viewing, interviewing, experimenting

Interpret: think from multiple perspectives, dialogue journals, paired discussions, debates

Respond: logs, journals, say something, pictures, dramatizations, movement

Invent: write directions, create machines, solve problems, write scripts, plan events

Explain: logs, journals, notes, literature circles, minipresentations, reports, essays, conferences

Create: scripts, book making, pictures, graphic organizers, poems, letters, newscasts, maps, time lines

Compare: literature circles, Venn diagrams, say something, debates, maps, think-alouds, multigenre writings

Perform: become the character, say something, read-alouds

Inform: news articles, brochures, books, posters, speeches, maps

Communicate: write, speak, question, debate, agree, disagree, share perspectives, share experiences, present information and ideas

Describe: essays, sketch to stretch, literature circles, glossary, pamphlets, posters

Infer: logs, intertextual essays, speeches, dramatizations, pictures, concept maps

Estimate: experiments, problem posing and solving, connecting with prior knowledge/experiences

Synthesize: graphic organizers, essays, using multiple references, sharing across texts

Relate: similarity and differences charts, this reminds me of…, notes, quick writes, KFN chart

Reason: think critically, give pros and cons, list the whys, use metaphors/analogies

CONCLUDING REMARKS ■

The element of stamina is often overlooked or noted as "time on task" in most of the reading-research literature. Our concept of stamina extends beyond time on task to include the ability to persevere when faced with more challenging or complex texts. The additional elements of our concept of reading self-efficacy—confidence, independence, and metacognitive abilities—helps create stamina in adolescent readers. At the same time, the ability to stay with a text and to complete an assignment—stamina—also produces more confidence and more independence in readers. It is when all these elements are working together that secondary readers build their reading self-efficacy and their reading proficiency. Chapter 6 more fully addresses how these concepts work together.

6

Developing Curriculum That Addresses Self-Efficacy

ADDRESSING SELF-EFFICACY IN THE CLASSROOM ■

"One of the things constantly in the zone of proximal development is our own self-image, including our beliefs about what we will and will not be capable of doing in the future."

—F. Smith, 1998, p. 85

Foundational to all learning is the sense within each learner that she or he desires to learn and can and will learn. This sense becomes an integral part of the success (or failure) each student meets when engaging in academic learning in classroom settings. More often than not too many students lack confidence, independence, metacognition, and stamina as the result of failed instruction, not because they lack the capability to succeed. Labels such as *lazy*, *stupid*, and *insolent* are too often applied to students who lack C-I-M-S because of teachers and administrators trying to fit them into the instructional boxes demanded by No Child Left Behind and high-stakes testing. We need to be creating instructional/learning opportunities that meet each learner where he or she is while providing learning communities that foster engaged, vibrant, excited, and enthusiastic learners. The four efficacy elements (C-I-M-S) discussed in this text are the major elements at work in both enabling students and encouraging students to make academic learning their own.

In order for teachers to facilitate the continuous development of their students' self-efficacy, especially confidence, independence, metacognition, and stamina, they need to create learning-centered classroom communities in which the instruction and engagements meet the needs of a wide variety of learners. To create a learning-centered classroom community, teachers need to plan using the three Rs—rigor, relevance, and relationship (Weeks, 2003).

In learning-centered classrooms, learning goals are negotiated with students, plans of study are outlined, and support for reaching the learning goals is provided by the teacher and the collaborative efforts of the peer group. In this way, learning-centered classrooms built around the three R's value and put the differences in background, interest, and development that each student brings to the community to good academic use.

Learning-centered classrooms facilitate the development of lifelong learning, which is needed in our twenty-first-century world. As Weeks (2003) pointed out, the Gates Foundation believes,

> To succeed as adults, they [children] will need, more than ever before, to think critically, work collaboratively, and be self-motivated. They will need technical and personal skills they can apply to new situations—the rate of change in today's working world spins ever faster. (p. 24)

C-I-M-S are key ingredients in a student's ability to develop a repertoire of leaning strategies to keep up with the fast-paced changes. In the following discussion, we present four factors which we believe to be vital in creating learning-centered classroom communities. Embedded within each of the four is the guidance afforded by the three Rs—rigor, relevance, and relationship. As we discuss the importance of the four factors—(1) curricular and instructional models; (2) text sets of multiple print materials; (3) choice and voice; and (4) sustained time for reading, writing, talking, thinking, and demonstrating learning—it is our hope that the reader will keep in mind the strategies recommended for each of the four self-efficacy elements—confidence, independence, metacognition, and stamina.

Curricular and Instructional Models

Models that call for planning content instruction around big ideas (Wiggins & McTighe, 2005) with many ways of exploring, building knowledge and understandings, and demonstrating learning are key. The goal for each and every student is to be working at the top of Bloom's taxonomy. When big ideas become foci rather than specific pieces of information, teachers can provide for the variety of backgrounds and skills that students bring into their classrooms.

Rigor

To establish and maintain rigor, teachers will need to begin instruction where each student is and facilitate each student's growth and development in an uninterrupted flow from the known to the new (Csikszentmihalyi, 1999; M. Smith & Wilhelm, 2004). For example, students are not only learning about the environmental impact of auto emissions on various ecosystems—they are connecting a synthesis of the new knowledge with what they already bring to the table such as an understanding of how cars work, an interest in global warming, or an interest in the development of biodegradable fuel. Thus, students are not only accessing prior knowledge; they are using it to make sense of new information and concepts.

Inquiry or project-based models (e.g., Fink, 2006; Freedman & Johnson, 2004) allow students to begin their pursuit of content knowledge and understanding from a point of adequate background and interest. From here, with teacher support and guidance through wide reading, writing, and discussing, students increase the complexity and depth of their study. Students become stronger readers and more confident, independent, metacognitive learners with expanded stamina.

Relevance

Inquiry and project-based models enable students to build purpose for the pursuit of reading and learning based on questions and ideas they want to explore. These models allow learners to make connections between the content under study and their own lives, interests, and desires. It is not enough for teachers to provide a purpose for learning or to acknowledge that students will need the information or skill when they are older. Relevance is now. Students need to care now. Using curricular and instructional models that enable students to engage with material now because it is interesting and connected is a key to authentic learning as well as the development of C-I-M-S, which supports that learning.

C-I-M-S development is predicated on the notion that learners feel that what they are doing is worthwhile. Being confident is predicated on having an intrinsic reason for pursuing a goal. Independence is founded on knowing how to pursue that goal. Metacognition is relied upon when the learner has reason to change or shift strategies in order to reach the goal. And stamina will only kick in when the learner has a driving need to reach a goal. All of these are predicated on the notion of relevance. When students ask "why are we doing this?" or "why are we learning this?" in a learning-centered classroom community where relevance is sought, a variety of answers are instantly forthcoming as each student takes a slightly different perspective on the answer, while they all collaboratively recognize the value.

Relationship

Inquiry and project-based models also allow more teacher time to be devoted to small groups and individuals. While the class is reading, writing, researching, or discussing, the teacher can be answering questions, modeling a specific strategy, encouraging active persistence, or providing ideas to pique interest among many other motivators.

Getting to know students is imperative in order to effectively guide learning. Teachers need to learn what their students' preconceived academic likes and dislikes are so that they can debunk these with authentic learning experiences. Teachers need to help students metacognitively access their knowledge base and connect their prior learning experience with what is currently being studied. They need to model these strategies for their students and freely ask and answer questions in a true give-and-take format.

Organizing the community of learners into small groups is an important tool for meeting the affective needs of students. Developing strategies that not only give students choice, but also allow teachers to manipulate the group compositions, are needed. For example, giving students three choices of projects that they would be willing to work on and assuring them that they will get one of the three, allows teachers some leeway to put certain learners together or keep others in separate groups.

Text Sets of Multiple Print Materials

Text sets of multiple print materials consist of a group of books, journals, and other print artifacts that all focus on a similar content concept, topic, or theme. The purpose of a text set is to

- validate each student's development level;
- spark interest, questions, and engagement;
- offer information from a variety of perspectives;
- offer information in a variety of genres and contexts;
- provide visual elements that reinforce and deepen concept understanding;
- support district curriculum as primary texts or as supplementary texts;
- reinforce the interrelatedness of reading and writing (as well as speaking, listening, and thinking); and
- provide avenues for authentic assessment and evaluation (Freedman & Johnson, 2004).

Rigor

Establishing text sets of multiple materials (e.g., Fink, 2006; Freedman & Johnson, 2004; Short & Harste, 1996) as the primary print materials for units of study in learning-centered classrooms addresses the individual needs of each student. Students can use this range of materials to continue to build intrinsic purposes for reading. For example, if students are studying about the era of World War II, print and electronic materials that are accessible to each student's reading level, interest, background, and purpose can be provided. Students who do not view themselves as readers may need texts that offer support in the form of graphics, lists, photographs with captions, glossaries, indices, and so forth. Students who think they hate history may need texts that are instantly engaging, that get them asking questions, and that leave them wanting more. Students who know very little about the World War II era, both in the United States and in Europe, may need materials that provide some background in connected, grounded ways that link this era to contemporary times. By the same token, students who come with a driving interest in the era of World War II and who have already studied this time period can access and use more of the complex and difficult materials in the text set to continue their learning. Many of the learners will be navigating across this range of material as they move further and further into the unit of study.

Self-efficacy depends on rigor for the continuous development of C-I-M-S because all learning depends on students being appropriately challenged and then supported to meet the demands of that challenge. In other words, learners are in a perpetual state of disequilibrium that relies on C-I-M-S as stabilizing forces in the pursuit of knowledge, understanding, and critical analysis.

Relevance

Having a variety of materials allows students to make connections and view events and concepts through multiple lenses. Providing many print materials for students to use to read about the content under study allows students to pick the material most relevant to their needs and goals.

Relationship

Providing multiple materials allows students to develop relationships with books, authors, and so forth. Getting to know certain authors or publishers and recognizing styles of writing can be an effective way for students to develop C-I-M-S. Learning how to use specific criteria to critique and assess print materials can be empowering and make students feel fully engaged in the work of the academic learning community. Learners with C-I-M-S readily and purposefully use support materials in books and Web sites such as glossaries, indices, tables of contents, notes, reference lists, and so forth. Further, they are eager to engage in conversation and discussion with their peers about the learning process they are using as well as the content under study.

Choice and Voice

Choice and voice are learning community elements that provide opportunities for students to negotiate learning activities within the constraints of the curriculum and content standards. The two of these go hand-in-hand, as it is as important for students to vocalize their ideas and desires and share their perspectives as this often leads to the development of the list of learning activities that they will use to make individual choices. For example, students could brainstorm and then choose from the following kinds of assessments: essays, posters, graphic organizers, logs, power notes, debates, dramatizations, newspaper articles, maps, proposals of solutions to problems, scripts, comic strips, and newscasts, among many others.

Rigor

The most important factor in a learning-centered classroom that fosters the development of C-I-M-S is the choices provided to each learner and then used by each learner to negotiate these choices. It is imperative that students have choice and voice in negotiating the ways in which they pursue learning and through which they demonstrate that learning. It is through this use of choice and voice that expectations can be raised and challenges can be met.

Relevance

Through the open and vocal negotiation of choices, relevance is recognized and connections are deepened. Student ownership of the work that they engage in is essential to their seeing the immediate reward of the learning they acquire. For example, in a study of ecosystems, students might decide that creating models of the various systems will be the way they delve into the subject, acquire the information needed, and share their learning.

Relationship

Teachers get to know their students better by negotiating with them. Giving students a voice in the work of the classroom only strengthens the relationships that are necessary for teachers to plan appropriately for students' continuous learning and development of C-I-M-S. The power of negotiation becomes visible in students learning to work with others, sharing information, building ideas together, and putting information together to create ideas and understandings.

Sustained Time for Reading, Writing, Talking, Thinking, and Sharing

Rigor

The rigorous pursuit of learning is dependent on the learner being given sufficient time to engage with the content to be learned. Instead of lectures, brief textbook sections, comprehension questions, worksheets, and multiple-choice tests, all of which disrupt the continuous and recursive flow of learning, learners need to engage with accessible, interesting texts in purposeful ways. They also need to demonstrate their ongoing learning through such mechanisms as journals, multigenre (Romano, 1995) projects, experiments, research, and so forth.

Assessment practices should also be rigorous and demanding so that students demonstrate continuous growth and development in their learning. If the starting point is where the child can engage easily with the material then C-I-M-S will increase as the student excels in academic achievement.

Relevance

Ample opportunity to practice authentic strategies for learning provides sustained time for students to make the necessary connections with content.

Relationship

Students should be provided with plenty of time to get to know each other and the materials through deeper connections. Revisiting print materials provides students with opportunities to gain wider perspectives and think critically. Rereading builds confidence, promotes independence, provides practice for metacognition, and reinforces the development of stamina.

WHERE DO WE GO FROM HERE? ■

Our C-I-M-S model of self-efficacy is foundational to students as they initiate, build, and demonstrate academic learning. Our focus needs to remain in two important arenas if the development of C-I-M-S is to be addressed in all classrooms. First, teachers need to engage in teacher/action research that addresses the role of self-efficacy in their classrooms. Second, the academic community needs to work in partnerships to provide for relevant, continuous professional development and coaching for teachers to learn and adapt strategies that support the development of C-I-M-S.

References

Angell, C., & Bates, P. (1996). Commonly encountered challenges and self-help solutions on the road to literacy: Ways to foster self-determination. *Reading Improvement, 33*, 143–147.

Au, K. H. (1997). Ownership, literacy achievement, and students of diverse cultural backgrounds. In J. T. Guthrie & A. Wigfield (Eds.), *Reading engagement: Motivating readers through integrated instruction* (pp. 168–182). Newark, DE: International Reading Association.

Baker, L. (2001). Metacognition in comprehension instruction. In C. Block & M. Pressley (Eds.), *Comprehension instruction: Research-based practices* (pp. 274–289). New York: Guilford.

Baker, L., & Brown, A. L. (1984). Metacognitive skills and reading. In P. D. Pearson (Ed.), *Handbook of reading research* (pp. 353–394). New York: Longman.

Bandura, A. (1986). *Social foundations of thought and action: A social cognitive theory.* Englewood Cliffs, NJ: Prentice Hall.

Bandura, A. (1994). Self-efficacy. In V. S. Ramachaudran (Ed.), *Encyclopedia of human behavior* (Vol. 4, pp. 71–81). New York: Academic Press.

Bandura, A. (1997). *Self-efficacy: The exercise of control.* New York: Freeman.

Baumann, J. F., & Duffy-Hester, A. M. (2002). Making sense of classroom worlds: Methodology in teacher research. In M. Kamil, P. B. Mosenthal, P. D. Pearson, & R. Barr (Eds.), *Methods of literacy research* (pp. 1–22). Mahwah, NJ: Lawrence Erlbaum Associates.

Baumann, J. F., Joes, L. A., & Seifert-Kessell, N. (1993). Using think alouds to enhance children's comprehension monitoring abilities. *The Reading Teacher, 47*(3), 184–193.

Beck, I. L., McKeown, M. G., Hamilton, R. L., & Kucan, L. (1997). *Questioning the author: An approach for enhancing student engagement with text.* Newark, DE: International Reading Association.

Berliner, D. C., & Biddle, B. J. (1995). *The manufactured crisis: Myths, fraud, and the attack on American public schools.* Reading, MA: Addison-Wesley.

Billingsley, B. S., & Wildman, T. M. (1990). Facilitating reading comprehension in learning disabled students: Metacognitive goals and instructional strategies. *Remedial and Special Education, 11*, 18–31.

Block, C. C. (2004). *Teaching comprehension: The comprehension process approach.* Boston: Allyn & Bacon.

Block, C. C., & Israel, S. E. (2004). The ABC's of performing highly effective think alouds. *The Reading Teacher, 58*, 154–167.

Csikszentmihalyi, M. (2000). *Beyond boredom and anxiety: Experiencing flow in work and play*. San Francisco: Jossey-Bass.

Cummins, C., Steward, M. T., & Block, C. (2005). Teaching several metacognitive strategies together increases students' independent metacognition. In S. E. Israel, C. C. Block, K. L. Bauserman, & K. Kinucan-Welsh (Eds.), *Metacognition in literacy learning* (pp. 299–314). Mahwah, NJ: Lawrence Erlbaum Associates.

Dewey, J. (1963). *Experience and education*. New York: Macmillan.

Duffy, G. (2005). Developing metacognitive teachers: Visioning and the expert's changing role in teacher education and professional development. In S. E. Israel, C. C. Block, K. L. Bauserman, & K. Kinucan-Welsh (Eds.), *Metacognition in literacy learning* (pp. 299–314). Mahwah, NJ: Lawrence Erlbaum Associates.

Fink, R. (2006). *Why Jane and John couldn't read—and how they learned: A new look at striving readers*. Newark, DE: International Reading Association.

Flavell, J. H. (1979). Metacognitive and comprehension monitoring: A new era of cognitive developmental inquiry. *American Psychologist, 34*, 906–911.

Frager, A. (1993). Affective dimensions of content area reading. *Journal of Reading, 36*(8), 616–622.

Freedman, L., & Johnson, H. (2004). *Inquiry, literacy, and learning in the middle grades*. Norwood, MA: Christopher-Gordon Publishers.

Gambrell, L. (1996). Creating classroom cultures that foster reading motivation. *The Reading Teacher, 50*(1), 14–25.

Garner, R. (1994). Metacognition and executive control. In R. B, Rudell, M. R. Rudell, & H. Singer (Eds.), *Theoretical models and processes of reading* (4th ed., pp. 715–732). Newark, DE: International Reading Association.

Georgiou, N. (1999). Parental attributions as predictors of involvement and influences on child development. *British Journal of Educational Psychology, 69*, 409–429.

Goodman, Y. (1996). Revaluing readers while readers revalue themselves: Retrospective miscue analysis. *The Reading Teacher, 49*(8), 600–609.

Grifith, P. L., & Ruan, J. (2005). What is metacognition and what should be its role in literacy instruction? In S. E. Israel, C. C. Block, K. L. Bauserman, & K. Kinucan-Welsh (Eds.), *Metacognition in literacy learning* (pp. 3–18). Mahwah, NJ: Lawrence Erlbaum Associates.

Harris, T. L., & Hodges, R. E. (Eds.). (1995). *The literacy dictionary*. Newark, DE: International Reading Association.

Horner, S., & Shwery, C. (2002). Becoming an engaged, self-regulated reader. *Theory into Practice, 41*(2), 102–109.

Jacobs, J., & Paris, S. (1987). Children's metacognition in reading: Issues in definition, measurement, and instruction. *Educational Psychologist, 22*, 255–278.

Katims, D., & Harmon, J. (2000). Strategic instruction in middle school social studies: Enhancing academic and literacy outcomes for at-risk students. *Intervention in School and Clinic, 35*(5), 280–289.

Kucer, S. B. (2005). *Dimensions of literacy: A conceptual base for teaching reading and writing in school settings*. Mahwah, NJ: Lawrence Erlbaum Associates.

Lipka, J., & McCarty, T. (1994). Changing the culture of schooling: Navajo and Yup'ik cases. *Anthropology & Education Quarterly, 25*, 266–284.

Marshall, J. (2001). Critical literacy and visual art: A living experience. In L. Ramirez & O. M. Gallardo (Eds.), *Portraits of teachers in multicultural settings: A critical literacy approach* (pp. 87–103). Boston: Allyn & Bacon.

McCray, A. (2001). Middle school students with reading disabilities. *The Reading Teacher, 55*(3), 298–300.

Opitz, M. F., & Rasinski, T. V. (1998). *Good-bye round robin: 25 effective oral reading strategies.* Portsmouth, NH: Heinemann.

Oster, L. (2001). Using the think aloud for reading instruction. *The Reading Teacher, 55,* 65–69.

Pajares, F. (2004). *Overview of social cognitive theory and of self-efficacy.* Retrieved October 26, 2004, from http://www.emory.edu/EDUCATION/mfp/eff.html

Paris. S. G., Lipson, M. Y., & Wixon, K. K. (1983). Becoming a strategic reader. *Contemporary Educational Psychology, 8,* 2144–2316.

Pearson, D., & Gallagher, M. (1983). The instruction of reading comprehension. *Contemporary Educational Psychology, 8,* 317–344.

Piaget, J. (1973). *To understand is to invent: The future of education.* New York: Grossman.

Romano, T. (1995). *Writing with passion: Life stories, multiple genres.* Portsmouth, NH: Boynton/Cook.

Rosenblatt, L. M. (1938). *Literature as exploration.* New York: Modern Language Association.

Sanacore, J. (1999). Encouraging children to make choices about their literacy learning. *Intervention in School and Clinic, 35(1),* 38–42.

Sanacore, J. (2000). Promoting the lifetime reading habit in middle school students. *The Clearing House, 73*(3), 157–161.

Santa, C. M. (2006). A vision for adolescent literacy: Ours or theirs? *Journal of Adult and Adolescent Literacy, 49*(6), 486–476.

Schoenbach, R., Greenleaf, C., Cziko, C., & Hurwitz, L. (1999). *Reading for understanding: A guide to improving reading in middle and high school classrooms.* San Francisco: Jossey-Bass.

Schon, D. (1983). *The reflective practitioner: How professionals think in action.* New York: Basic Books.

Short, K. G., Harste, J. C., & Burke, C. (1996). *Creating classrooms for authors and inquirers* (2nd ed.). Portsmouth, NH: Heinemann.

Smith, F. (1998). *The book of learning and forgetting.* New York: Teachers College Press.

Smith, F. (2004). *Understanding reading* (6th ed.). Mahwah, NJ: Lawrence Erlbaum Associates.

Smith, J. L., & Johnson, H. A. (1993). Sharing responsibility: Making room for student voices. *Social Education, 57*(7), 362–364.

Smith, M., & Wilhelm, J. (2004). "I just like being good at it": The importance of competence in the literate lives of young men. *Journal of Adolescent & Adult Literacy, 47*(6), 454–461.

Swafford, J., & Bryan, J. (2000). Instructional strategies for promoting conceptual change: Supporting middle school students. *Reading & Writing Quarterly, 16,* 139–161.

Tobin, K. (1984). Student task involvement in activity oriented science. *Journal of Research in Science Teaching, 21,* 469–482.

Tovani, C., & Losh, S. (2003). Motivation, self-confidence, and expectations as predictors of the academic performances among our high school students. *Child Study Journal, 33*(3), 141–151.

Vygotsky, L. (1978). *Mind in society: The development of higher psychological processes.* Cambridge, MA: Harvard University Press.

Wang, Y. (2000). Children's attitudes toward reading and their literacy development. *Journal of Instructional Psychology, 27*(2), 120–125.

Weeks, D. J. (2003). Rigor, relevance, and relationships: The three r's of the Bill & Melinda Gates Foundation. Retrieved January 13, 2007, from http://www.nwrel.org/nwedu/09-02/rigor.asp

Wiggins, G. & McTighe, J. (2005). *Understanding by design* (2nd ed.). Baltimore: Association of Supervision and Curriculum Development.

Wilhelm, J., Baker, T., & Dube, J. (2001). *Strategic reading: Guiding students to lifelong literacy, 6–12.* Portsmouth, NH: Heinemann.

Williams, M. (2001). Making connections: A workshop for adolescents who struggle with reading. *Journal of Adolescent and Adult Literacy, 44*(7), 588–602.

Worthy, J., & Broaddus, K. (2002). Fluency beyond the primary grades: From group performance to silent, independent reading. *The Reading Teacher, 55*(4), 334–343.

Zeichner, K., & Liston, D. (1985). Varieties of discourse in supervisory conferences. *Teaching and Teacher Education, 1*(2), 155–174.

Index

CORWIN PRESS

The Corwin Press logo—a raven striding across an open book—represents the union of courage and learning. Corwin Press is committed to improving education for all learners by publishing books and other professional development resources for those serving the field of PreK–12 education. By providing practical, hands-on materials, Corwin Press continues to carry out the promise of its motto: **"Helping Educators Do Their Work Better."**